BLOODY B
HISTO

C000253299

LEEDS

BLOODY BRITISH HISTORY

HISTORY

LEEDS

RICHARD SMYTH

First published in 2013

The History Press
The Mill, Brimscombe Port
Stroud, Gloucestershire, GL5 2QG
www.thehistorypress.co.uk

© Richard Smyth, 2013

The right of Richard Smyth to be identified as the Author
of this work has been asserted in accordance with the
Copyrights, Designs and Patents Act 1988.

All rights reserved. No part of this book may be reprinted
or reproduced or utilised in any form or by any electronic,
mechanical or other means, now known or hereafter invented,
including photocopying and recording, or in any information
storage or retrieval system, without the permission in writing
from the Publishers.
British Library Cataloguing in Publication Data.
A catalogue record for this book is available from the British Library.

ISBN 978 0 7524 8737 3

Typesetting and origination by The History Press
Printed in Great Britain

CONTENTS

THE BATTLE FOR BRIGANTIA

THE ROMANS ARRIVED in Britain in the year AD 43; they'd made a previous visit under Julius Caesar just less than a hundred years earlier, but that 'invasion' barely got north of the Thames and can therefore be dismissed as little more than a sight-seeing trip. At this time, the region we now know as Yorkshire was occupied by a tribe of hill-dwelling proto-Yorkshiremen known as the Brigantes, who had come over from Continental Europe in a series of invasions dating back to the fourth century BC.

The Brigantes weren't sure what to make of these road-building, fort-obsessed immigrants. Some liked their style, and established diplomatic links with the Roman governor Ostorius Scapula. Others, less cosmopolitan in outlook, resented the newcomers. Add to this mix a handful of the Welsh border-folk called the Silures, and you have an explosive brew indeed.

In AD 51, eight years after the Roman conquest began, the brew began to fizz. The catalyst was called Cartimandua.

Cartimandua was the queen of the Brigantes and the leader of the pro-Roman faction. When Caratacus,

chieftain of the Silures, came to her seeking protection, Cartimandua showed herself to be a true politician: she clapped him in irons and delivered him up to the Romans.

This didn't go down well with Venutius, a formidable Brigantian warrior chief who was famed for his fierce hatred of the Romans. It was unfortunate, therefore, that he happened to be Cartimandua's husband...

The ensuing marital tiff soon escalated into all-out guerrilla warfare throughout Brigantia. Venutius established an anti-Roman resistance force. In retaliation, Cartimandua kidnapped his family. It soon became evident that a reconciliation was not on the cards. Venutius departed to the Dales, and Cartimandua sought refuge among the Romans: their marriage was over (though it's not known whether the official divorce paperwork was ever completed).

Venutius and his Brigantes went on to begin the construction of a monumental system of forts and defences a little way north of Richmond in North Yorkshire. However, in the year AD 74, the Roman army of Petillius Cerialis unsportingly

Above *Map of Roman
Britain. Caratacus fled from
the kingdom of the Silures
to that of the Brigantes –
where he was betrayed by a
warrior queen. (THP)*

Right *Caratacus pleading
for his life amongst the
Romans. (THP)*

arrived before the Brigantes were ready, and Venutius's people were driven into the wilderness: those that didn't escape and weren't killed in the fighting probably went on to unrewarding careers as slaves in the Romans' lead mines.

Petillius Cerialis soon made himself at home in the old Brigantian capital of Isurium (now Aldborough, near Boroughbridge). A new era had begun. Brigantia was no more.

Cerialis was replaced soon enough by Sextus Julius Frontinus, who himself got the boot in favour of Agricola in the year 78. Agricola, understandably suspicious of the Brigantes still lurking in the hinterland between York and the Tyne, pondered the situation and finally hit on a solution that only a Roman would think of: he would not wage war; he would build roads!

The construction of the roads from outpost to outpost – Chester to the Solway, Aldborough to Manchester, York to Ribchester, and many others – would have been heavily reliant on the labour of enslaved Brigantes. Agricola's implacable tramp northwards was not *entirely* without violence – Romans were almost as keen on subduing rebellious natives as they were on building roads – but, as one historian has noted, the new governor was 'gentle as the breath of June' to those who sought only peace with the Romans.

When Agricola was done, the landscape of northern England was not only spanned by new roads but also pocked with Roman fortresses.

So presumably Leeds had one of the grandest of all? Something in keeping with its status as Yorkshire's first city? It has a train station and a Harvey Nichols,

after all. You would think it would be the first place the Romans would head to (if only to grab a spot of dinner or to take in a show in between oppressing Brigantes).

But the curious thing about the Romans is that seem to have come to Britain without even the most rudimentary local guidebook. They pretty much bypassed Leeds entirely. Instead, they chose to visit such improbable spots as Castleford, Sowerby and the town that they called Olicana, and that we today call Ilkley. (Ilkley is now best known for its part in what Yorkshire folk regard as their 'national' anthem and everyone else regards as incomprehensible gibberish: 'On Ilkey Moor Baht 'At', a nineteenth-century dialect song in which a young man is warned that, by going courting on the titular moor, he runs the risk of dying horribly from pneumonia and being devoured by worms. Strange, you might think, that such a song has been taken to the hearts of a people as carefree, laidback and cheerful as Yorkshire folk are universally known to be.)

Ilkley, now very much the smaller cousin of the Leeds-Bradford conurbation, had a fort of its very own – and it was no mere ornament. Though fairly small, intended to house only an infantry cohort, it saw plenty of action – serious action.

In 115, the North erupted in revolt against the Roman occupation. The fort at Ilkley – then only a wooden construction – was stormed by the Brigantes and burnt down in the violence. The uprising was so fierce that the Romans felt it necessary to bring troops from mainland Europe in order to subdue (and then punish) the rebels. In the course of these troubles, the IXth Legion at nearby York was either eliminated or somehow disgraced – all we know is that it was replaced in the city the Romans called Eboracum by the VIth Legion.

The dogged Romans rebuilt the fort at Ilkley, this time (sensibly) in stone. But a generation later, the Brigantes were at it again; again they rose up in revolt – again (helped out this time by marauders from north of Hadrian's nice new wall) they destroyed the fort at Ilkley.

When, in 155, the Romans finally succeeded in stamping out this uprising, they were so pleased about it that they had some special commemorative coins minted. They shouldn't have bothered, because in 197 the death of Governor Claudius Albinus triggered yet another outbreak of anti-Roman violence. Ilkey was assaulted yet again; yet again, the fort was knocked about by the Brigantes and their northern allies.

Peace, of a sort, arrived eventually. The years between 200 and 300 were relatively untroubled, and Roman Britain prospered.

It wouldn't last.

One day in the late third century, the Romans in coastal East Yorkshire looked out across the bleak grey expanse of the North Sea, the eternal barrier between Continental Europe and the islands of Britain, and saw ships cutting through the white-edged waves. Pirate ships. The ships of men from beyond the North Sea, of the men of the tribes of the North German plains – the men known as *Saxons*.

The Yorkshire coast was savagely plundered in pirate raids throughout the final years of the fourth century. The Romans, distracted and weakened by intrigue in their Continental heartlands, were in no condition to resist – particularly as the Pictish and Scottish tribes of the North launched attack after attack across the now-abandoned Hadrian's Wall.

In 410, the Roman Empire had its heart torn out: the Visigoths, rampaging south from their Germanic homelands, put the city of Rome to the sword. The few Romans left in Britain withdrew, shattered and demoralised, to the south. From Scotland and from the sea, a new invasion force swarmed into Yorkshire.

Leeds would eventually flourish amid the savagery – but, with the Empire in ruins and the Saxons rampant, there would be no Romans left in Britain to witness it.

RIVER OF BLOOD

PEOPLE WERE FIGHTING battles over Leeds before Leeds was even Leeds. And these were no petty squabbles: the Battle of Winwaed, for instance, was a clash of Christianity and paganism that would decide the destiny of two great kingdoms.

Centuries before the Civil War, Britain was a land divided. The Anglo-Saxon kings had divided the country into a 'heptarchy' of four powerful kingdoms (Wessex, Mercia, Northumbria and East Anglia) and three slightly-less-powerful kingdoms (Kent, Sussex and Essex). But that makes things sound more neat and orderly than they really were. It was a time of conquest and re-conquest, uneasy alliances and violent border skirmishes.

In November 655, the tensions between the kingdoms came to a head. Penda, pagan king of the Midland kingdom of Mercia, was on the rampage. He and the Northumbrian kings had a bloody history. In the summer of 642, Penda's army had smashed the Northumbrians at Maserfield in Shropshire; Oswald, king of Northumbria, had been killed in the battle – and, afterwards, messily dismembered by the Mercians.

Things like that create bad blood. In 655, when Penda and his Thirty Warlords marched north in a bid to consolidate their supremacy, Oswy, Oswald's brother, was there to face him.

Oswy, sensibly, wasn't exactly spoiling for a fight with his brother's butchers. First he tried to pay them off – but the pagan Penda was having none of it. The Mercian king wanted to finish what he'd started at Maserfield, and destroy the Northumbrians 'from the highest to the lowest'.

The Mercian forces laid siege to a Northumbrian stronghold at Iudeu, near modern-day Stirling. It isn't clear how or why the siege was lifted. Tradition says that Oswy, having failed to bribe Penda, instead tried to bribe God instead, pledging to send his daughter to a nunnery and to establish a dozen monasteries – and that God accepted. Historians suspect that, in fact, he renewed his offer of 'an incalculable quantity of regalia and presents' to Penda, and that it was Penda who at last relented, ended his siege, and turned south.

Whitby Abbey, founded as payment for victory at Winwaed. (Courtesy of the Library of Congress, LC-DIG-ppmsc-09080)

At which point, Oswy regathered his armies and set off in pursuit.

The armies of the two kingdoms clashed at the River Winwaed in November 655. The Winwaed flowed to the north-east of modern-day Leeds, near the suburbs of Whinmoor and Crossgates. It would have been a muddy as well as a bloody scene: heavy rains had swollen the Winwaed and turned the banks of the river to bog. Penda's men, weary from their campaign in the far north, were ill-prepared for further fighting. What was worse, the Welsh forces under Cadafael ap Cynfeddw who had accompanied them to Idueu had now left for home. In fact, some said that they had sneakily abandoned their allies in the night, leaving the Mercians to face the Northumbrians alone – a rumour that earned Cadafael the nickname 'Cadomedd', or 'battle-shirker'. Another so-called ally of the Mercians, Œthelwald of Deira, son of the late King Oswald, also edged out of the battle.

The Northumbrians, though outnumbered, fell savagely on the Mercians. Exhausted, betrayed, demoralised, foundering in the mud, the Mercian army broke, and ran – only to find the roaring River Winwaed blocking their escape. 'Many more were drowned in the flight,' reported the historian Bede, 'than destroyed by the sword.'

Penda, though, was certainly destroyed by the sword: the last of the great pagan kings had his head hacked off by a Northumbrian warrior. His Thirty Warlords also fell at Winwaed, as did his ally King Æthelhere of East Anglia. The Winwaed, it was said, ran with blood – and the brutal death of King Oswald was avenged.

Winwaed was a turning point in the history of Britain. The long-waning twilight of Anglo-Saxon paganism was finally snuffed out; Christianity, the faith of Oswy, overtook Mercia. Oswy kept his promise to God: twelve monasteries were indeed founded in the wake of the battle (the one at Whitby is perhaps the most famous).

The miserable scrap on the boggy Leeds riverbank also, indirectly, created a saint: it is said that Hereswitha, the sister of St Hilda of Whitby, became a nun – and, eventually, a saint – only after her beloved husband was slain at Winwaed.

Early Christians in Britain: the religion was fostered by the Christian King Oswy. (THP)

THE TWO KINGS

Penda

Penda, the pagan overlord of Mercia for some thirty years, was the scourge of the Northumbrian kings: as well as Oswald, slain and cut into pieces at Maserfield, Penda had seen off his uncle, King Eadwine, killed at Hatfield Chase in 633. After that battle, Eadwine's son, Eadfrith, went over to the Mercians – only to be murdered at Penda's command. Penda had also butchered three kings of East Anglia in his savage assaults to the east. He was the terror of the Christian kingdoms – and England's last great pagan king.

Oswy

Oswy had been exiled from Northumbria as a young boy by his uncle, King Eadwine. He had grown up in Scotland and Ireland with his brothers, Oswald, Oslac, Oswudu, Oslaf, Offa and Eanfrith. Possibly an illegitimate child himself, when he returned to Northumbria as king he fathered at least seven children – with three different women. After Winwaed, Oswy took control of a vast swathe of northern Britain, imposing Northumbrian rule on, among others, the Mercians to the south and the Picts to the north; no English king would rule such a vast kingdom until the accession of James I almost 1,000 years later.

AD 1070

HUNTED DOWN AND BUTCHERED

– By Their Own King!

THE HISTORY OF the area we now know as 'Leeds' began with what was in some ways a lucky escape – and, in others, one of English history's darkest and most blood-soaked episodes.

When, in October 1066, William the Conquerer (aka William, Duke of Normandy, aka William the Bastard) defeated the army of Harold II at Hastings, it was not so much the beginning of the end as the end of the beginning. William's Christmas Day coronation established the Bastard as king in the minds of the invading Normans. But the men and women of England had other ideas.

And it wasn't only England. Denmark, the historic occupier-cum-ally of England, lurked just beyond the kingdom's boundaries, keen to unsettle the French usurper. These were difficult times for William. They weren't easy for the occupied English, either: the men appointed by William to rule the country (while he popped home to Normandy), Bishop Odo of Bayeux and William FitzOsbern, soon became bywords for oppression and mismanagement.

The first mutterings of revolt were heard in the West Country. In 1068,

Exeter boldly refused to submit to the new king. The Norman response was emphatic: the city was attacked and besieged. When hostages were surrendered to William by a Normanite faction within the city walls, the Conqueror had one blinded and the other hanged. Surrender soon followed. The south-west was subdued. Now William was forced to look north.

In spring 1068, according to the *Worcester Chronicle*, William was informed that 'the men of the North were gathered together and meant to make a stand against him'. The Anglo-Saxon kingdom of Northumbria, which ranged from the Humber to the Tees, had not yet seen any sign of the invaders' army; the Conqueror, it was supposed, could be parleyed with, bargained with, and, in effect, ignored.

They would soon learn otherwise. The

William the Conqueror.
(THP)

Normans, with the Conqueror at their head, began the long march north. This was not a royal procession; it was a military advance.

The Northumbria-bound force paused *en route* to flex its muscles in the Midland kingdom of Mercia. Here, under the leadership of the Anglo-Saxon Earl Edwin, the natives had been growing restless. The arrival of the formidable Normans put a stop to that.

One of the central pillars of the Norman *modus operandi* was the construction of castles – lots of castles. The Norman *motte* wasn't just a practical precaution; it was a powerful, if unsubtle, psychological statement. Such a fortress would dominate the countryside for miles around, especially in flat regions such as Lincolnshire and the fens. It could support a substantial garrison of knights, archers and men-at-arms. Wherever a Norman castle was built, the message was clear: *we're in charge now*.

Norman castles at Lincoln, Nottingham and (possibly) Leicester were enough to cow the Mercians into submission and obedience.

And so to Northumbria.

In the marshes of the West Riding, Maerleswain, the exiled sheriff of Lincolnshire, had been busily building fortifications in preparation for an uprising. The Northumbrians planned to make their stand on the Aire-Humber frontier: if they could stall the Normans for long enough, reinforcements would surely arrive from Mercia, or perhaps Denmark.

Such resistance was a pipe-dream.

William's attack was fast and fierce. Northumbria was simply not prepared: its ineffectual ruler, Earl Cospatric, fled to Scotland; when the Conquerer entered York, it was as though there had never been a rebellion.

At York, the Normans built their most imposing fortress yet, damming the River Foss and flooding a large area of the city to provide their *motte* with a wide defensive moat. William's enemies were subdued. But it was an uneasy peace indeed.

YORKSHIRE'S SILVATICI: THE ORIGINAL ROBIN HOODS

The wily Northumbrians, while not willing or able to confront the Norman invaders head-on, were not yet ready to knuckle under to the Conquerer. Instead, the rebels melted away into the wild Yorkshire countryside. They became what the chronicler Orderic Vitalis called *silvatici*: wild men.

Living rough, skulking in the deep woods and high hills, harrying the Norman occupiers through highway robbery and hit-and-run raids, the silvatici soon entered English folkore. These were the original Robin Hoods, the men who created the template of the brave-hearted forest outlaw.

In reality, though, these were not particularly Merrie Men. On the contrary, they were hard-bitten, savage, desperate and hell-bent on vengeance.

The silvatici would be a painful thorn in the Conquerer's side throughout the late 1060s.

The summer of 1069 saw the simmering anti-Norman feeling build to a violent climax. Durham, suffering under the brutal governance of Robert de Commines, rose up in revolt; the vicious warfare soon spread south, to York, where the uprising took as its figurehead Edgar the Aetheling, son of Edward the Confessor, Harold II's predecessor.

Wales, too, led by Prince Bleddyn, rose up against the Normans; rebellions broke out in Cheshire, Staffordshire and the south-west. Late in the summer, the Danes arrived: in a series of ruthless raids, they ravaged the coast of East Anglia and Kent.

The bloody risings shook the Normans. But even in Northumbria, where, at York in September, the Norman garrison was finally routed, the rebel triumph was not conclusive.

William's Norman gold bought peace with the Danes. York, crippled by fire, was soon re-taken. The Normans had not been driven out of the North. And now William the Bastard prepared to take his revenge.

No one in Northumbria – neither the native rebels nor the invading Danes – saw it coming. In February 1070, the Normans struck. This time they did not stop at York: William's target was St Cuthbert's Land, the far north-east that had been Northumbria's rebel heartland. The Conqueror's Norman soldiers rampaged as far north as the Tyne, taking no prisoners, giving no quarter, and showing no mercy. Jarrow Church was burned to the ground. The rebels fled; William ordered his men to hunt them down.

In the nine months that followed, the North was put to the sword. The viciousness of William's assault shocked even his Norman subjects. Heading south from Tyneside, the king had led his men over the bleak, wintry Pennines – a march of inhumane harshness, during which his men were reduced to eating the flesh of horses that drowned in the bogs – to savagely put down a rumoured rising in Chester. Norman troops ran wild in Shropshire, Staffordshire and Derbyshire, spreading ruin and starvation. This was just a taste of what the king had in store for the North.

From his base in London, the Conqueror ordered the Harrying of the North. Within a year, he had reduced more than a 100 square miles of his own kingdom to a bleak, windswept wilderness.

'He did not cease the whole winter,' wrote the monk and chronicler Simeon of Durham, 'from ravaging the country, slaughtering the men, and performing many other acts of ferocity.' Hugh the Chanter, of York, recorded that the whole district had been 'destroyed by the French with the sword, famine and fire'.

The Normans destroyed precious seed corn, condemning whole communities to starvation; animals were slaughtered, homes burnt down – even farming tools were smashed by the rampaging troops.

'He [the Conqueror] harried the land and burnt homes to ashes,' reported Orderic Vitalis.

Nowhere else had William shown such cruelty. In his anger he commanded that all crops and herds, chattels and food of every kind, should be brought together and burned to ashes with consuming fire, so that the whole region north of the Humber might be stripped of all means of sustenance.

Pigs, game and food of any kind was slaughtered and burnt, driving the North to the verge of starvation. (With kind permission of the Thomas Fisher Rare Book Library, University of Toronto)

In consequence, so serious a scarcity was felt in England, and so terrible a famine fell upon the humble and defenceless populace, that more than 100,000 Christian folk of both sexes, young and old, perished of hunger.

What we would now consider the suburbs of Leeds did not escape the Norman scourge: to the east, Seacroft, Garforth, Coldcotes, Halton and Manston; to the west, Bramley; to the south, Beeston; to the north, Allerton – all were utterly ruined. 'So great a famine prevailed that men, compelled by hunger, devoured human flesh, that of horses, dogs and cats, and whatever custom abhors,' reported Simeon of Durham.

Others sold themselves to perpetual slavery, so that they might in any way preserve their wretched existence; others, while about to go into exile from their country, fell down in the middle of their journey and gave up the ghost.

It was horrific to behold human corpses decaying in the houses, the streets and the roads, swarming with worms, while they were consuming in corruption with an abominable stench. For no one was left to bury them in the earth, all being cut off either by the sword or by famine, or having left the country on account of the famine.

By December, it was as though some virulent and lethal plague had swept through the land north of the Humber. The Conqueror's revenge was complete.

'I dare not commend him,' wrote Orderic Vitalis. 'He levelled both the bad and the good in one common ruin by a consuming famine... he was... guilty of wholesale massacre... and barbarous homicide.'

These were scars that would take a long time to heal. In 1086, sixteen years after the horrors of the Harrying, the Domesday survey set down in writing the value of the towns and villages of England. In the section dedicated to the North, estate after estate is characterised in a single word: *waste*. It's estimated that the population of Yorkshire was reduced to around a quarter of what it had been before the Conquest.

And yet... Leeds, somehow, survived. Amid the starvation and slaughter, the little town on the Aire, with its population of around 200, actually increased in value. This may be down to the city's good connections at court. The leading local landowner was the de Lacy family, favourites of the Conquerer; de Lacy lands in the Pontefract area also seem to have been spared.

So Leeds, like a resilient weed, continued to grow. The North, gradually, painfully, recovered. And it may be that William the Bastard, in the end, repented of his cruelty.

Orderic Vitalis, perhaps fancifully, recorded the penitent William's dying words: 'I... caused the death of thousands by starvation and war, especially in Yorkshire,' the Conqueror is said to have lamented on his Normandy deathbed:

In a mad fury I descended on the English of the north like a raging lion, and ordered that their homes and crops and all their equipment and furnishings should be burnt at once and their great flocks and herds of sheep and cattle slaughtered everywhere.

So I chastised a great multitude of men and women with the lash of starvation and, alas! was the cruel murderer of many thousands, both young and old.

Thus the final curtain came down on one of the bleakest episodes in the history of England. But the story of Leeds went on.

AD 1152

THE WANDERING WHITE MONKS

LIFE IS SELDOM comfortable when you're a monk. Lots of praying, lots of work, not much in the way of home comforts. But the modern-day monk has it relatively easy. When you're a monk in Dark Ages Yorkshire, life is *tough*.

The history of Yorkshire's Cistercian abbeys reads a little like a family tree, or perhaps like some sort of monastic relay-race. It all began in the history factory that is York, at St Mary's Abbey (large bits of which can still be found in the city's Museum Gardens). In 1132 the Benedictine monks at St Mary's started bickering over certain points of order. As so often when monks bicker, this soon escalated into a full-scale riot. Thirteen monks were politely asked to leave.

These monks were reformers. The Order of Benedict was just a little too comfy for them. These monks wanted to *suffer* in the service of their religion. And suffer they would.

On leaving York, the reformists were granted a plot of land by Thurstan, Archbishop of York. It wasn't what you'd call prime real-estate. The monks' new home was in the valley of Skell, in the wilderness to the west of Ripon. One

chronicler described the spot as 'more fit for wild beasts than men to inhabit' – but it had timber, and water, and shelter, and was therefore more than enough for the hard-as-nails followers of the new-fangled Order of Cistercians.

The abbey the exiles founded at Skell was accepted into the Cistercian Order in 1135. Cistercians were old school. Whereas the Benedictines of St Mary's had to some degree moved with the times, the Cistercians insisted on keeping it real: they demanded full and literal compliance with the Rule of St Benedict, laid down in around 500. The Rule is traditionally summed up in a simple phrase: 'Work and pray.'

Strenuous manual labour took up much of the time of the monks of Skell. They ate hardly at all, and spoke even less. Their monastic robes were nothing but cloaks of untreated sheep's wool – made particularly uncomfortable by strict rules prohibiting the wearing of underwear.

The monks' home in the Skell valley soon became known as Fountains Abbey. But for some, it would not remain home for long; for these monks, their destiny lay to the south.

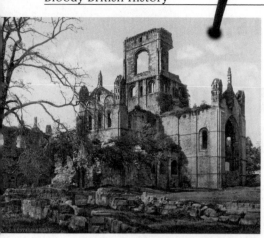

Kirkstall Abbey. (Courtesy of the Library of Congress, LC-DIG-ppmsc-09037)

A party of Cistercians left Fountains in 1147. Their destination was a new monastery, funded by local noble Henry de Lacy. It was in Barnoldswick (then Bernolfwic), a few miles north of modern-day Burnley. Few monks can ever have suffered like the Cistercians suffered at Barnoldswick.

For a start, it was freezing cold and rained incessantly. The monks almost starved. Roaming roughnecks stole or ruined their property (such as it was). And things got even worse when the monks tried to get tough with the local churchgoers.

In establishing their new home in Barnoldswick, the monks had driven out the local villagers, who seem to have taken this development in their stride – save for the fact that they insisted on returning to the site in order to attend church. The monks were not standing for this. Their solution was simple: they pulled down the church.

They then decided that it might be a good idea to skip town. They consulted de Lacy. Yes, he said, he had just the

place for them – a spot by the River Aire, not far from the town of Leeds. It was 'remote from the habitation of man', of course, but that was what the Cistercians wanted. And it already had a (supposedly) spiritual heritage: in the early 1000s, a visionary shepherd named Seleth was said to have wandered to Kirkstall from 'the south' and established his hermitage there.

So the site that would later be Kirkstall Abbey was cleared of its hermits, vagrants and other wildlife and settled by the monks in 1152.

The recently de-churched villagers of Barnoldswick, meanwhile, lodged complaints with the local Archbishop and, ultimately, the Pope about the high-handed conduct of the invading monks. The Archbishop and the Pope were both Cistercians. The complaints were ignored.

One of our best sources for the early history of Kirkstall Abbey is one 'Serlo', an elderly monk who, in the best traditions of Dark Age history, may or may not have existed. Hugh de Kirkstall, a Cistercian who was commissioned as the abbey's in-house chronicler, claimed that his history of the Fountains and Kirkstall Abbeys had in fact been dictated to him by Serlo, a veteran of the monks' Fountains Abbey salad days and of the Barnoldswick debacle: this Serlo describes himself in the history as 'a man now decrepit, as you see, and worn out with old age'.

This elderly Cistercian – who, if he ever lived, presumably died at Kirkstall – enjoyed a relatively peaceful existence with his fellow monks on the banks of the Aire. Like most monks of the day, the Kirkstall 'White Monks' were skilled and diligent craftsmen; metalwork was a particular speciality, and a formidable ironworks would be maintained at Kirkstall long after the monks were gone.

Another feature of the monks' existence may be surprising to those familiar with the Cistercian creed (but not, perhaps, those familiar with the history of church institutions down the ages). The White Monks were simply rolling in money.

By 1300, the abbey had acquired 216 draught oxen, 160 cows, 152 bullocks, and 4,000 sheep and lambs. By the 1530s, the White Monks were pulling in around £10,000 a year – excluding the value of their livestock and lands.

But the abbey's fortunes were also surprisingly erratic: while, under the governance of some abbots, the monks' pockets bulged, under others their finances were so cackhandedly managed that only the intervention of the king spared them a visit from the bailiffs.

The conduct of the Kirkstall monks was by no means atypical. Throughout the land, monastic orders were resented as neglectful and greedy landlords (not to mention unreliable payers). In the summer of 1535, Thomas Cromwell, vicar-general to Henry VIII, ordered a nation-wide inspection of England's monasteries.

The findings were not positive.

Henry, having read and digested the inspectors' reports, concluded that enough was enough. Why should monks and nuns be permitted to suck up the nation's wealth? That was *his* job. With a wave of the monarch's hand, 376 monasteries were dissolved; their holdings were seized by the Crown and sold off at fire-sale prices. At Kirkstall, the king's agents stripped the lead from the abbey roofs and the glass from the windows in order to deter the monks from returning; to make sure of the job, they also diverted the main road into Leeds so that it ran right through the abbey nave. And that was that for the Cistercians of Kirkstall.

But it was not quite the end of the story. Many people – particularly in the North – took the view that even a monastery that ripped off its tenants and stockpiled sheep was better than no monastery at all. The rebellion against the Dissolution actually began in Lincolnshire, but it was only when it was hijacked by Yorkshire lawyer Robert Aske that it acquired the evocative name by which it's now known – the Pilgrimage of Grace.

Aske gathered an army of sympathisers – including monks from Fountains Abbey – and marched from York to Pontefract in October 1536. Among his men was Leeds nobleman William Calverley (father of the murderous Walter, of whom more later). After taking the castle, they advanced – amid much busy politicking – to Doncaster, some 30 miles south of Leeds. There they parleyed with the king's man, Thomas Howard, Duke of Norfolk. Norfolk, negotiating in the face of 20,000 to 30,000 testy Catholic Yorkshiremen, struck a deal: no action would be taken against the rebels, and a parliament would be convened in York to discuss their demands.

Mollified, Aske and the other leaders of the Pilgrimage tore off their captains' badges, and the rebel army retreated.

Not for nothing does the Book of Common Prayer advise 'put not your faith in princes' – and the same goes double for kings.

In 1537, a new revolt broke out in Cumberland under the renegade noble Sir Francis Bigod. It had nothing to do with Aske, but it was all the excuse the king needed. Henry promptly executed a spectacular double-cross: around 215 prominent pilgrims – Aske included, plus dozens of monks, abbots and priests – were arrested and executed. Many were beheaded. Most were hanged. Some were hanged *and* drawn *and* quartered (that is to say, they were *hanged* from a rope, and, while they were choking, had their bellies sliced open and their bowels *drawn* out, before being sawn into *quarters*).

Poor Robert Aske was hanged in chains from the walls of York Castle. And the Dissolution of the Monasteries continued unabated.

Templar Knight. (With kind permission of the Thomas Fisher Rare Book Library, University of Toronto)

THE TAX-DODGING CRUSADERS OF WHITKIRK

The Cistercians at Kirkstall were not the only privileged order in the Leeds of the Middle Ages. The Knights of the Holy Grail also took more than their fair share.

The Grail – a key element of medieval Christian mythology – was said to be in the care of the Knights Templar, an order of religious knights founded at the time of the Crusades to protect Christian pilgrims in the Holy Land. Over time, the Templars became immensely powerful throughout much of Europe – Yorkshire not excepted. Temple Newsam, for example, takes its name from the chivalrous Grail-guardians, who maintained a community at nearby Whitkirk. They owned a lot of property in central Leeds too. Any building owned by the Templars was marked with a cross – a shorthand way of telling visiting tax-collectors where they could stick their Final Demands, because the Templars were exempt.

As the rules of the Templars' order required them to abstain from sex, gambling, swearing and drinking, they would probably not be best pleased to learn that now, 1,000 years later, they are commemorated in the name of a Leeds pub.

AD 1399

THE MURDERED KING AND THE FORGOTTEN CASTLE

LEEDS CASTLE IS one of the most beautiful post-Norman castles in England. Constructed in 1119, in the thirteenth century it became a favourite residence of Edward I; it was probably Edward who ordered the construction of the castle's formidable barbican and luxurious royal living quarters. In later years, it would play a key role in the diplomatic manoeuvrings of monarchs including Richard II and Henry VIII; today, it features a maze, a golf-course and – yes! – a dog-collar museum, and attracts more than 500,000 visitors every year.

It's just rather a shame that Leeds Castle is 200 miles away from the city of Leeds, in deepest Kent, and is therefore of no interest to us whatsoever.

But Leeds – the city, as opposed to the small Kentish village – does have a castle. Or at least it *did* have one.

It was either the Norman aristocrats the de Lacys of Pontefract or their Leeds sub-aristocrats the Paganels that oversaw the construction of 'the Castle of Leeds' (as chroniclers have traditionally called it in a futile attempt to avoid confusion with the Kent tourist-magnet). The castle occupied the Mill Hill-Boar Lane-Bishopgate area of the city centre; a Norman who fell asleep in the keep and awoke around a millennium later would probably find himself in the public bar of the Scarbrough Hotel, or thereabouts. It's thought that Park Square and Park Row may take their names from the castle's extensive grounds. There was a moat, too: labourers digging out warehouse

A view of Leeds Castle, Kent. (SXC)

23

foundations uncovered its ancient workings in 1836.

One Leeds antiquary of the nineteenth century wrote – in what we might call an extended educated guess – that the castle 'gave dignity, importance and protection to the town; and enabled lords, with the usual habit of feudal despotism, to domineer over their serfs and slaves'.

But then, this same antiquary – one Edward Parsons – was one of a whole parade of helplessly confused Victorian scholars who got their Leedses mixed up and, to give just one example, transposed the fierce 1139 siege of Leeds Castle by King Stephen from rural Kent to urban Yorkshire. Our antiquary cites the fact that Stephen besieged the castle of Leeds as evidence that the city was 'a place of consequence and strength' – and it might well have been, if he had, but he didn't, so it's not.

To be fair to these fuddled savants, Stephen, in the course of his war with the Empress Matilda, *had* recently been in the area, slaughtering Matilda-ite Scotsmen at the Battle of the Standard at Northallerton in 1138. But Professor Edmund King, the country's leading scholar of Stephen's reign, confirms it: there's simply no evidence that he stopped off at Leeds on his way there.

At some point in the early Middle Ages, the castle at Leeds fell into ruin, and was broken up. Here's Parsons, our imaginative Leeds antiquary, again: 'It may have been abandoned by its proprietors to the violence of the tempest, to the ravages of time, and the fury of hostile invasion; and its materials may have been applied by the growing population of the town to the construction of other buildings of

Park Row, named after the vanished castle's parklands. (THP)

convenience, or commerce, or religion, until the walls of the once proud and formidable edifice were completely subverted, and their very foundations effectually concealed beneath the ruins and accumulations of ages.'

One of the city's oldest legends maintains that the stones from the castle were in fact used to build Leeds Bridge, the historic thoroughfare across the River Aire. This might indeed be the case – but, if it is, it discredits yet another semi-legendary tale of the Castle of Leeds.

In 1399, King Richard II, ruler of England for more than twenty years, was deposed. Richard, an ambitious but somewhat incompetent king, had always had a turbulent relationship with both Parliament and the people – not to mention his own family. In the end it was his cousin, Henry Bolingbroke, who turfed him off the throne to become Henry IV.

Richard's abdication (made somewhat at sword-point) came in September. The ex-king spent the next few months being shuttled from prison to prison, until, early in 1400, a cabal of his former courtiers were caught out in a plot to restore him to the throne.

Henry could not stand for this. Even in chains, the deposed king was a threat to his authority. Richard was quite simply too dangerous to be allowed to live.

But the end did not come quickly.

Richard, just turned thirty-three, had been held captive in Pontefract Castle, just over ten miles south-east of Leeds, since before Christmas 1399. He had been transported there by his captors from the Tower of London – and, before checking in at his final destination, had spent a single uneasy night in the dungeons of the wintry Castle of Leeds.

Or possibly the castle at Knaresborough, fourteen miles north. Or maybe both. No one knows.

We aren't even sure how Richard met his death at Pontefract (or, as Shakespeare had it, Pomfret). According to Shakespeare, he was hacked to death by Sir Piers Exton while battling valiantly with his captors ('Exton, thy fierce hand hath with the king's blood stain'd the king's own land'). According to less excitable commentators, his demise was far less glorious: some say that he was cruelly deprived of food, and starved to death; others maintain that his slow starvation was self-imposed.

Either way, by the end of the winter, he was dead.

Parsons prefers to believe that Richard did indeed stay at the Castle of Leeds on his way to this melancholy end – or 'barbarous murder', as Parsons puts it. In doing so, he debunks the legend of Leeds Bridge, for the bridge has been standing since at least 1376.

So Leeds can have Richard, shivering in his cell in fear of his life in the depth of the Yorkshire winter, or it can have a bridge founded on the ancient stones of a ruined castle – but it can't have both.

But what it *does* have, somewhere deep down below the shops and pubs and buses and traffic of the modern-day city, is the memory of a remnant of a ruin that was once, without doubt, the Castle of Leeds.

AD 1605

SLAUGHTER AT CALVERLEY HALL

WALTER CALVERLEY WAS a tormented man. The heir to properties throughout West Yorkshire, he was nevertheless subjected to a form of bondage: under the terms of his father's will, Walter was the ward of a nobleman, a relative of Baron Cobham. In around 1580, this hard-nosed noble ordered Walter into a marriage of convenience to Philippa Brooke – regardless of the fact that the young man was privately betrothed to a local landowner's daughter.

A hack named George Wilkins later turned this unhappy episode into a well-known play entitled *The Miseries of Enforced Marriage*. It was not the last drama Walter Calverley's sad life would inspire.

Walter and his wife lived miserably together at Calverley Hall, a grand, stony residence in the deep valley between Horsforth and Eccleshill. Walter sought solace in riotous living: 'diceing, drinking, revelling, and it is feared other things,' as one contemporary noted. Poor Philippa, secluded and far from home (she had been brought up from London by her dissolute new husband), was left to look after the couple's three sons, William, Walter and Henry.

Money spilled through Walter's hands like water: vintner's bills, gambling debts, lavish household expenses. His inheritance was squandered; Philippa's dowry, too, was soon spent. Walter's creditors moved in: his land at Pudsey, Seacroft and elsewhere was confiscated. The Calverleys were bankrupt.

What was worse, Walter's younger brother William, who had stood surety for the Calverley estate, was arrested.

Walter heard the news on 23 April 1605. Maybe he was drunk. Maybe debt and depression had driven him out of his senses. All we know is that something inside him snapped.

Walter's four-year-old son William was playing in one of the galleries of Calverley Hall when Walter drew a dagger and stabbed him three times. Walter then grabbed the dying, bloodied child and dragged him into Philippa's bedroom. Philippa was asleep; a nurse was feeding the couple's second child, Walter.

The horror that Philippa must have felt on awakening, finding at the foot of her bed her wild-eyed husband clutching the bloodied body of her eldest son, is unimaginable. Her reaction must have been instinctive: to protect her other child.

It was not, however, enough. Walter Calverley fought off Philippa and the nurse and rammed his dagger into the body of the nursing baby. Then he turned on his wife: he slashed at her savagely, inflicting severe wounds.

Walter Calverley murdering his family, as depicted in an illustrated volume of Shakespeare's plays. (THP)

He dashed from the hall and ran for his horse. His destination was obvious: the nearby village of Calverley, where one-year-old Henry, the Calverleys' sole surviving child, was in the care of a nurse. Walter seems to have been resolved to complete his terrible work.

He never made it. His horse stumbled, and he was thrown into the road. A servant, sent from the hall in pursuit, apprehended him.

The last, dark chapter of Walter Calverley's life began.

Two local magistrates heard Walter's confession the next day. The reason he gave them for murdering his sons was confusing. His wife Philippa, he claimed, had on several occasions 'uttered speeches and given signs and tokens' that William, Walter and Henry were not in fact his children; moreover, 'he had found himself to be in danger of his life sundry times by his said wife'. The idea of murdering the boys, he admitted, had been in his mind for some two years.

The news must have chilled the neighbourhood. These were bleak times for the people of the wild country between Leeds and Bradford. At around the same time as the horror at Calverley Hall, four villagers had been certified by the vicar of Calverley as being 'vehemently suspected of the *devilish art* of *witchcraft*'. Tensions were high; nerves were on edge.

Walter Calverley's trial, too, was conducted in an atmosphere of fear and unrest. Sentenced to prison in York, he had instead been interned at Wakefield – for York was then in the grip of a plague that by the summer's end would claim more than 3,500 lives.

27

A YORKSHIRE TRAGEDY

Shortly after Walter's arrest, a Leeds jour-nalist named Nathaniel Butter rushed out a pamphlet describing the terrible events that had taken place at Calverley Hall. The account he gave inspired not only Wilkins' *The Miseries of Enforced Marriage*, but also a play by a rather better-known writer.

A Yorkshire Tragedy was included in both the 1664 and 1685 folio editions of the works of Shakespeare. In it, the Bard grue-somely dramatizes the murder of William as he plays with his whip and top: 'Bleed, bleed, rather than beg!' He recreates the stabbing of the babe-in-arms Walter ('Brat, thou shalt not live to shame thy house!'), the assault on Philippa ('The surest way to charm a woman's tongue, is break her neck!') and the headlong flight in pursuit of little Henry ('Now to my brat at nurse, my sucking beggar: Fates, I'll not leave you one to trample on!').

Except, of course, that *A Yorkshire Tragedy* isn't by Shakespeare at all. Attaching Shakespeare's name to a play was a sure way of selling more copies – but the disappointing truth is that the play is in fact a piece of hack-work, probably by Thomas Middleton or Thomas Heywood.

The story remains, however, a tragedy. And the play's subtitle – 'Not so New as Lamentable' – continues to ring true.

But eventually Walter was brought in chains to the disease-racked walled city. In court, charged with murdering Walter and William and attempting to murder Henry and his wife Philippa, he pled neither 'guilty' nor 'not guilty' – he remained obstinately silent. Under the law of the day, the land and titles of a defendant who refused to plead could not be forfeited. By his silence, Walter sought to secure an inheritance for Henry – the child he had damned as another man's son; the child he had ridden so wildly to Calverley to kill.

Walter's obstinacy would be severely tested. The England of 1604 was a barbarous place. This was the kingdom of the witch-hunt, the pillory and the ducking-stool, a land in which a gossip might have her tongue pierced through with a skewer or a vagrant a brand burned into his skin with a red-hot iron. If Walter Calverley refused to plead, the courts had ways of making him talk.

The practice of *peine forte et dure* originated in England in the thirteenth century. Originally a non-lethal punishment or penance for prisoners

Peine fort et dure. (THP)

who refused to appear before a jury, by Walter Calverley's day it was a terrible fate indeed. A prisoner was condemned to *peine forte et dure* if he or she, like Walter, was 'obstinately mute'. He or she would be, to use the English term for the sentence, 'pressed to death'.

In a York prison cell Walter was stripped of his clothes and chained, spread-eagled on his back, to a cold stone floor. On his breast was laid a wooden board; on the board was laid a great weight of iron or stone.

We don't know how long Walter Calverley endured the torture. It could have been a matter of hours or days. He would have been fed, if he was fed at all, on rotten bread and stagnant water. We don't know how great the weight was that bore down mercilessly upon him – burdens of 400lb and more were not unknown. We don't know if his executioners, in a common act of 'mercy', hastened his death by placing a sharp stone or chunk of timber beneath his body.

But we do know that he endured it in silence. He did not plead. He died on 5 August 1605. His title and remaining estate passed to Henry, the only remaining Calverley boy.

AD 1645

'THOU SHALT DIE, NOT LIVE'

The Plague Comes to Leeds!

THE HISTORIAN PAUL SLACK has pointed out that, in the England of the 1600s, towns were, above all, places where people died.

One of the many reasons for this was 'the Pestilence' or 'the Mortality' – the plague.

The disease, known scientifically as *Yersinia pestis*, was a recurring horror for medieval city-dwellers. The disease began with a flea-bite. Next came shivering, then vomiting, headache, giddiness, and intolerance to light. The victim suffered terrible pain in the back and limbs. Sleeplessness, apathy, or delirium followed.

Most terrible of all – the surest sign that this *was* the dreaded plague – were the 'buboes', horrible swellings of the lymph glands that erupted in the armpits and groin. Or a victim might suffer from pneumonic plague, which struck at the lungs, causing a boiling fever and causing the victim to cough up blood.

Whether the plague was bubonic or pneumonic, death was the most common consequence.

The people of the Leeds region were given a fearful lesson in the horrors of pestilence in the fourteenth century,

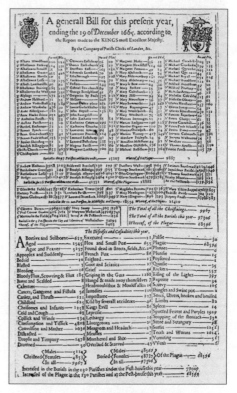

One of the famous 'Bills of Mortality' for London. This one is from 1665, one of the plague's most virulent years. The bill lists 68,596 deaths from the disease in capital alone; five other Londoners were 'blasted', twenty-three were 'frighted', one poisoned, and 2,614 died of 'teeth and worms'. (THP)

when the Black Death ravaged the west. It's thought that around 25 million people perished in Europe from the plague, which arose in the Crimea in 1347. In 1348 it made landfall in England: a ship docked at Melcombe in Dorset carried a Gascony sailor in the throes of the disease. From Dorset the plague spread to Bristol, then England's second city, and a vibrant trading port. The plague brought the city to its knees.

In London, where it raged throughout the winter of 1348 and on into 1349, it took the lives of almost half the population. Flea-ridden, rat-infested, stinking and filthy, England's cities fell like dominoes to the ravages of the Black Death.

Yorkshire was no exception. Thousands were consumed by the plague in 1349.

When the Black Death finally subsided in 1350, England was a quieter and emptier place. Farmsteads stood abandoned. Church bells tolled in deserted town squares.

In a curious way, it was all very good news for the town of Leeds. The crippling shortage of workers – so many lost to the devouring plague – meant that labour was at a premium. In the short term, wages went up. In the longer term, communities learned to adapt. One change that many made was to give up growing crops on their land – back-breaking work that was highly labour-intensive – and, instead, turn it over to pasture for sheep. Sheep meant wool. The plague had sown the seeds for the industry on which the future city of Leeds would be built.

Over the course of the next few centuries, this great city, as it grew,

would always find that its economy was intimately tied up with its health – or, rather, its sickness. Leeds got bigger, and it got richer, but it didn't get any cleaner. Perhaps it suffered from the same complaint as London had during the Black Death: ordering the city to clean up its filth, King Edward III had been chasteningly told that this could not be done – as all the street-cleaners were dead from the plague.

Leeds' foul and murky streets were hothouses for the cultivation of disease. And disease, when it struck, took with it mill-workers, weavers, farmers, merchants and dyers – it took with it the city's livelihood. Dozens died with each visitation of the plague; when it flared up again, in 1597, the death-toll reached 311.

In the 1630s, having seen how plagues had crippled the mining industry of the north-east and the farming industry of the south-west, Yorkshire aristocrat and land baron Sir Thomas Wentworth fretted about the prospect of a similarly damaging pestilence wreaking havoc among

One unlikely outcome of the Black Death: pasture land was turned to grazing land for sheep, beginning Leeds' rise to prosperity. (With kind permission of the Thomas Fisher Rare Book Library, University of Toronto)

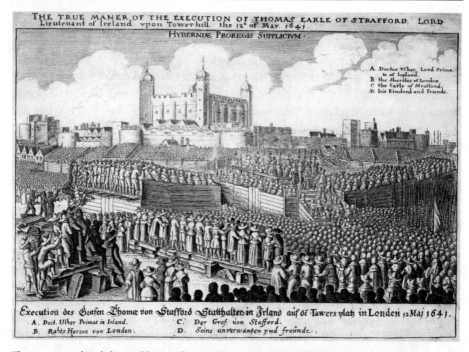

The execution of Yorkshire nobleman Thomas Wentworth, Earl of Strafford. A decade before he had fretted that a Leeds plague would 'mightily distress and impoverish' his estates. (With kind permission of the Thomas Fisher Rare Book Library, University of Toronto)

those who toiled on his own estates. The arrival of a major Leeds plague, he mused nervously, would 'mightily distress and impoverish' the whole of the West Riding. Wentworth, beheaded in 1641 as the country plunged into Civil War, did not live to see it – but in 1645, the Leeds plague struck.

This was a 'plague year': Oxford, Lichfield, Derby and Bristol all suffered from the pestilence in '45. In Leeds, its arrival was marked by uncertainty: it was reported that 131 people fell dead 'before the plague was perceived', suggesting that this strain of the disease was so fiercely virulent that sufferers died (horribly) from septicaemia – blood poisoning – even before the tell-tale 'buboes' had formed in their armpits and groins.

By mid-March, though, there could be no doubt. The plague had broken out in Vicar Lane, in the east of the town centre; one Alice Musgrave was its first 'official' victim.

Before long, according to the contemporary historian Gideon Harvey, 'the market-place and streets in the town were covered with grass'; in a matter of months, the terrible epidemic had struck down some 1,300 people – around a fifth of the population. The plague seethed in the narrow streets of the Calls, Mill Hill and Lower Briggate. Vicar Lane remained its godforsaken epicentre.

On 2 July, 'the ould church doores was shut up and prayers and sermons onley at Newchurch', a restriction that remained in place until the following Easter.

AD 1642–1643

TOM FAIRFAX'S WAR

The Taking of Leeds, the Slaughter on the Moor, and the Miracle at Wakefield

THE ENGLISH CIVIL WAR, which erupted in 1642, tore the nation apart for nine long years and left the soil of England steeped in the blood of its sons and daughters. What began as a power struggle in Westminster and ended only after terrible slaughter on the fields of Marston Moor, Adwalton and elsewhere is often remembered as a clash between King and Parliament, Cavaliers and Roundheads – but the roots of the conflict ran deeper than that.

In many ways, the battlefield on which the Civil War was fought was religion. The mid-1600s was a time of heretics and radicals, wild-eyed visionaries and ragged-voiced preachers. Ranters raved against the established church and Levellers demanded the overthrow of privilege and private wealth. The provinces of England simmered in a foment of religious dissent. It would take more than a final, weary, blood-soaked Parliamentarian victory at Worcester in 1651 to dispel this profound sense of alienation.

King Charles, of course, was the figurehead of the Royalists; the 'Roundheads' who rallied to the Parliamentarian cause will always be associated with Oliver Cromwell. But in Yorkshire, the war was all about one man: Sir Thomas Fairfax.

Fairfax was born in Denton, just outside Ilkley, in 1612. A career soldier, he earned his spurs leading the Yorkshire dragoons against the Scots in 1639 (a follow-up campaign in 1640 was less successful: Fairfax and his men were routed at Newburn, Northumberland, and Fairfax confessed that his knees did not stop trembling until he was safely south of the Tees). King Charles knighted the gallant Yorkshireman in 1641. Perhaps he was trying to secure Fairfax's loyalty; if so, the tactic failed.

In the high summer of '42, with the country on the brink, Charles travelled to Heworth Moor, near York. Fairfax, at the head of a group of local gentry, was there to meet him. Barging his way through the king's entourage, Fairfax presented Charles with a petition outlining the people's demands. Charles refused it, and rode disdainfully away.

S. THOMAS FAIRFAX
Generael van de Armee van de Parliament van Engellandt, A° 1648.
W. Hollar f.,   EV Wyngs, excud. Antverpia.

Above *Thomas Fairfax. (With kind permission of the Thomas Fisher Rare Book Library, University of Toronto)*

THE MOST HIGH AND
Mighty Prince CHARLES by the Grace of God, King of England, Scotland, France and Ireland, defendor of the Faith.

Right *Charles I. (With kind permission of the Thomas Fisher Rare Book Library, University of Toronto)*

Within three months, Thomas Fairfax was serving as second-in-command to his father, Lord Fairfax, commander of the Parliamentary army.

Leeds had its first brush with the war when Fairfax's small force at Wetherby was taken by surprise (it was said that the Parliamentarian sentries had been asleep) by an 800-strong Royalist detachment. Fairfax fought fiercely at the head of his badly outnumbered force. When the Royalist officer Major Carr fell in the thick of the fighting, the stunned Royalists fell back, regrouped – and readied to attack once more. But as they advanced – certain

now, it seemed, to take the town – the Parliamentarians' magazine, ignited by a stray spark, exploded. The horror and carnage was great: seven of Fairfax's men were killed by the blast. But the horrendous noise, flame and stink of gunsmoke convinced the Royalists that the Parliamentarians somehow had cannon at their disposal – and, understandably, fled.

Fairfax had earned his first victory.

The bitter fighting went on in the Parliamentarian heartlands of industrial West Yorkshire. At Tadcaster, a blistering assault by the Earl of Newport's Royalists drove Fairfax's massed forces into retreat. At Bradford, a Royalist siege was repulsed amid horrible violence as townsmen armed with flails, clubs, scythes and halberds wrought havoc in the king's ranks.

As 1642 drew to a close, however, the Royalists had the upper hand in Yorkshire. The Royalists' northern army, under the Earl of Newcastle, was a force far more formidable than the Fairfaxes could muster. By December, Leeds, Wakefield, Skipton, Knaresborough and York were all in the hands of the king's men.

Thomas Fairfax and his army arrived in Bradford from Tadcaster at Christmastime, around 1,000 strong. The general's objective now was straightforward: to take the city of Leeds. Only the small matter of 2,000 Royalist soldiers stood in his way.

Fairfax summoned Roundheads from Halifax and Bradford as he prepared for the assault. It began in the south, amid heavily falling snow: a company of dragoons led thirty musketeers and a brigade of 1,000 'clubmen' – that is, men armed with clubs – to the brink of the Aire, taking up position just across the bridge from the Royalist-held town. The main force, meanwhile, crossed the river at Apperley bridge, around 7 miles upstream. From there they marched to Woodhouse Moor in the north of the town, where the university now stands. Here they issued their ultimatum to Sir William Saville, second-in-command of the Yorkshire Royalists. The message was clear: give up the town, or have it taken from you.

Skipton, which fell during the Civil Wars. (Courtesy of the Library of Congress, LC-DIG-ppmsc-09071)

Slaughter re-enacted: a musket volley by the Sealed Knot. Thirty musketeers led the assault on Leeds. (Charles Drakew)

Tadcaster Bridge, which could not be taken by Fairfax. (Tim Green)

But Saville, confident in his numerical advantage and backed up by two cannon, declined.

Fairfax had identified the western edge of Leeds as the Royalists' weak spot, and it was here, along a line of fortifications running from St John's church (now on New Briggate) to the river, that the Parliamentarians now attacked. Musketry roared as the two sides engaged; acrid smoke turned the air grey, and blood stained the fresh-fallen snow.

For two hours the two sides battled fiercely for the town. Then, at last, a breakthrough: the Royalist fortifications were breached. Soon after, they gave way again, at a point further south – and the west of the town was in the hands of the Roundheads.

Now the force arrayed on the Aire's south bank began its advance across the river. The Royalists' line of retreat was blocked – the only way to go was east, to the far end of Kirkgate, to where the parish church stood. Saville's men, reduced to a rabble, fled there in panic. Many, feeling Fairfax's breath on the backs of their necks, made for the river; some swam to safety; some were drowned.

When the musket-smoke cleared, twenty-eight Royalists and twelve Parliamentarians lay dead. All – it's easy to forget – were English soldiers. Fairfax rounded up the remaining Royalists. Around 500 were taken prisoner.

The battle for Leeds was over; it was Fairfax's greatest victory yet. But beyond the town, the war continued to rage. The weary Parliamentary army could not rest on its laurels. The fight must, of course, go on.

Fairfax's next target was Tadcaster, the town to the north from which he and his army had been driven by the Royalists the previous year. Key to the town was the bridge over the River Wharfe, which controlled the main road westward. If the bridge could be destroyed, the town would be at his mercy.

The bridge, it turned out, could not be destroyed. Thus began Thomas Fairfax's darkest hour.

Back went the Parliamentarians, retreating southward into the bleak, open wilds of the West Riding. They were a town army, composed of town men and musketeers, designed for gun-fights and close-range combat. As they crossed Bramham Moor, wide-open to the gusting spring winds, they must have felt intensely vulnerable – for all the reassuring presence of the great Fairfax, the hero of Leeds.

And their fear must have been terrible when they heard the thunder of Lord Goring's Royalist cavalry approaching across the barren, featureless plain of Seacroft Moor.

They were strung-out and exposed, and still a good 4 miles from the safety of Leeds (the home town of many of the men – one can only imagine how they longed to see it at that moment). They had only a token cavalry force; even pikemen, who at least stood a sporting chance against men on horseback, were in short supply.

Goring's men ripped into them like a cannon broadside.

Fairfax lost around 1,000 men in the slaughter. In a chilling echo of the long-ago battle on the nearby Winawaed, it was said that Cock Beck,

Cock Beck, which ran red with blood. (THP)

the stream that crossed the dismal moor, ran red with the Roundheads' blood.

Fairfax stumbled back to Leeds, accompanied by the remnants of his cavalry and speaking bleakly of 'the greatest loss we ever received'. But there was a bright side to be discerned among the gloom: his failed assault on Tadcaster had allowed his father's troops to make a dash from beleaguered Selby to the security of Parliamentarian Leeds. The Fairfaxes and their bloodied Roundheads could rest and regroup.

Then they could plot their next attack.

Now Thomas Fairfax's strategic focus was on the manufacturing heartland to the south of their stronghold on the Aire. Wakefield, the city on the Calder, was his

target. Only 800 or 900 Royalist soldiers were stationed there; Fairfax could count on some 1,500 men. The odds would surely be on the Parliamentarians' side.

It was to be a surprise attack: by marching through the night, Fairfax hoped to catch the Royalists napping. But at some point on the 9-mile march south, word reached the general that his information was not quite accurate. There were more than 900 Royalists at Wakefield – in fact, there were 3,000. And there would be no surprise attack: the Royalists were ready and waiting for them.

But the army was by now too far advanced – there was no turning back.

Later in the war, stories were told of Fairfax plunging into battle with the cry: 'Let us fall on; I never prospered better than when I fought against the enemy three or four to one!'

If the general ever did say those words, he surely had the taking of Wakefield in mind at the time. This was the feat that cemented Fairfax's reputation – 'Fairfax, the man most beloved and relied upon by the rebels in the north', as one Royalist put it.

The Roundheads attacked at dawn, Fairfax leading from the front. Parliamentary infantry stormed the city barricades, forcing three breaches in two hours of intense combat. Fairfax saw his chance and took it: as the Royalist defences faltered, the general led a cavalry charge through the barricades and into the streets of Wakefield.

He must have been bewildered, minutes later, to realise that the clattering hoofbeats of his cavalry comrades had died away – that he had ridden too hard, and left his fellows behind. He was quite alone, and surrounded by Royalist infantry, in Wakefield market square.

But derring-do was what Fairfax did. He spurred his horse, leapt a barricade, and re-joined the general fighting. The Roundheads' momentum was unstoppable. Even as Lord Goring, the victor of Seacroft, staggered fever-ridden from his bed to lead a counter-attack, Fairfax's men were turning captured artillery on the city's defenders. A second cavalry charge shattered the Royalists altogether. The battle was over; the ailing Goring was among the 1,500 king's men taken prisoner. Another of Yorkshire's great cities had fallen to General Thomas Fairfax.

But a great general can only do so much. Of course, the Parliamentarian cause was to triumph in the end – but, with their northern army hopelessly outnumbered by Newcastle's Royalists,

Westgate, Wakefield, in around 1900. (THP)

that final victory must have seemed far from inevitable, even to the dauntless Fairfax.

In 1643, it was still three years away (or eight, depending on your definition). Before it came, all of Tom Fairfax's bold and bloody work in Yorkshire would be undone.

Occupying Wakefield was all well and good, but it left the Roundheads stretched dangerously thin across West Yorkshire. Fairfax was summoned back to Leeds: his father needed him. Newcastle was on the march. Twelve thousand men, it was said, were advancing on Bradford. It seemed that a great reckoning was not far away.

What followed was the last stand of the Fairfaxes in Yorkshire. Adwalton Moor, south-west of Bradford, was the appointed place. The army that they led there was outnumbered by the Royalists by two to one.

And at first it seemed that Tom Fairfax's luck might yet hold. The Roundheads fought bravely and cleverly among the hedgerows of the heath. The right wing of the army, under Sir Thomas, may even have been on the point of breakthrough – when the left, under Lord Fairfax, gave way. The game was up.

Lord Fairfax's routed men returned broken to Bradford. Sir Thomas had a harder time of it: he and his men somehow fought their way through the Royalist blockades to reach first Halifax and then – after a desperately exhausting 6-mile forced march – to Bradford.

But their hold on the town was precarious at best. They could not stay – but to leave would place them, their families and their men in the gravest peril. The Fairfaxes took the only course open to them.

On the night of 1 July, Lord Fairfax led the greater part of the Roundhead army out of Bradford, and headed in haste to the only sure Parliamentarian redoubt left in the north: Hull, some 60 miles to the east. Sir Thomas and his wife and daughter stayed behind with a small cavalry force to help cover the retreat.

Two days later, they made a break for it too. But on the Leeds road they ran into trouble: a detachment of 300 Royalist cavalrymen.

Most of the Roundheads were unceremoniously butchered. Lady Fairfax was taken prisoner; Sir Thomas, somehow, escaped, and, with the bare handful of troopers who had likewise survived the slaughter, made his way into Leeds. There were Parliamentarians there – some stragglers from Bradford and Adwalton, plus a small garrison left by Lord Fairfax – but they could not remain for long. A twenty-hour march eastward lay ahead of them.

In the course of this journey – the last chapter of his first Yorkshire campaign – Sir Tom Fairfax contrived to rout the Royalists at Selby, get shot through the wrist, fight a running battle as he led his troops along the broadening River Humber, and, finally, escort his father and the remnants of the northern Parliamentary army into the safe-haven of Hull.

But the war was far from over – and the man who took Leeds in the name of Parliament had not fought his last battle on Yorkshire's soil.

RAISING THE DEAD IN LEEDS

1733
Workers digging a well at Carlton, south-east Leeds, were startled to unearth a vast tomb some 8ft underground. Within were the bones of a tall man, 'white as ivory' and surmounted with a warrior's helmet. Saxon characters scratched on the wall of the sepulchre recorded the date: 992, seventy-four years before the Norman Conquest.

1790
A gang of workmen digging for clay in the George Street area of Leeds made a grisly discovery: a cluster of fifty oak coffins, each containing mouldering human bones. They were thought to date from a plague outbreak of 1672, when some 1,400 people were buried in the area.

1823
During the construction of a new road from Hunslet to Bell Isle, workers uncovered a stone coffin. Levering off its heavy lid, they found thigh, leg and arm bones, all covered with plaster. The plaster carried the imprint of the shrouded body that had long since rotted away. Teeth and glass beads were also found in the bottom of the coffin.

1849
The workers who disinterred a large Saxon coffin from the mud of Addle Mill Farm in Leeds must have had high hopes of what lay within. A king's gold? A warrior's loot? The coffin was certainly impressive, 7ft long and 2ft wide. They opened it up – and found 'nothing except a small quantity of dark-looking mould'.

1852
These were surely the strangest bones ever found in Leeds. At Longley, near Wortley, workmen turned up a clutter of peculiar animal remains. They were not from cows or horses. No, explained an expert from the Leeds Philosophical Society. They were from *Hippopotamus major*, the Great Northern Hippopotamus. This mighty beast, very like a modern hippo but with a shaggy coating of hair, roamed the swamps of what would later be Leeds in the Pleistocene era – 2.5 million years ago.

The epidemic reached its horrendous peak in the last week of July, when 216 people succumbed. Each was listed in the parish registers with the note *de peste* – of the pestilence.

The plague 'so infected the air,' Harvey reports, 'that the birds fell down in their flight over the town'. This persistent legend is highly unlikely to be true: birds are immune to infection with *P. pestis*.

It may well be true, however, as other chroniclers noted, that 'dogs and cats, rats and mice' also died in great numbers during that hot, stinking summer.

At Quarry Hill – then a little way out of town – the townspeople erected 'plague cabins', in which victims were confined in an attempt to prevent the infection from spreading. It was probably – in those days before even the most

What remains of Allerton Hall, Chapel Allerton. According to the Leodis website, John Harrison, the noted Leeds benefactor, sought sanctuary from the plague here in 1645.

basic principles of germ control had been established – a futile effort. In the years afterwards, these bleak localities were nicknamed 'Cabin Closes'.

In the churches of the town, those hardy preachers who had not fled the pestilence did a brisk trade putting the fear of God into anyone not already sufficiently mortified by the sights, smells and sufferings all around them. Robert Todd of St John's, for instance, preached sermons from the Old Testament book of Isaiah: 'In those days was Hezekiah sick unto death,' he told the congregation, 'and Isaiah the prophet the son of Amoz came unto him, and said to him, Thus saith the Lord: set thine house in order, for thy shalt die, not live.'

Hezekiah, in the Bible, is cured by a combination of divine intervention and Isaiah placing 'a lump of figs' on his boils. It would take more than that to heal the suppurating buboes that swelled in the armpits and groins of the terrified people of Leeds that summer. The local physicians' efforts – the usual charade of blood-letting and bowel-purging – did little better.

Historian Whitaker notes, however, that 'I cannot discover that any person of name in the town died of the plague'. It was just poor people – those who lived in filth and squalor, and lacked the means to escape when the plague struck – who perished in their hundreds. No one famous. No one *we* know. So that's all right then.

The plague never returned to Leeds with such ferocity (though the darkness of the Industrial Revolution would bring new and terrible scourges to the city). Ten years afterwards, however, Leeds' foremost historian, Ralph Thoresby, recalled that a strange 'distemper' – a violent, uncontrollable cough – attacked not only Leeds but all of the North. By now hardened to sickness, the people not only endured this new disease but gave it a nickname: 'the Jolly Raut', in the old sense of a 'raut' or 'rout' meaning to bellow or roar.

'I was too young or inobservant to make such remarks as might be of use,' Thoresby recalled, 'but very well remember that it affected all manner of persons ... so universally that it was almost impossible to hear distinctly an entire sentence of a sermon.'

Little use, in that case, in reminding the city's churchgoers of Hezekiah, his boil, and the healing properties of a lump of figs.

AD 1663

TREASON AND PLOT AT FARNLEY WOOD

EVEN AFTER THE ROYALIST triumph of the Restoration, which brought Charles II to the throne in 1660, resentment and fear continued to smoulder in many corners of the war-ravaged kingdom.

Farnley Wood, a region of thick forest on the south-west edge of modern-day Leeds, was one such corner. On a rain-drenched October night in 1663, a dramatic story of conspiracy, rebellion and betrayal was played out here.

It would not end happily.

This part of Yorkshire had long been the northern heartland of the Parliamentarian cause. The 1643 Battle of Adwalton Moor – just a little way to the south-west of Farnley – had broken the back of the Parliamentarians' military resistance in the region, but the wounds it had left still festered.

Captain Thomas Oates had not fought at Adwalton, but he had served the Roundhead cause with distinction elsewhere. At Winceby, Nantwich and Marston Moor, he had ridden in the bloody cavalry charges ordered by Sir Thomas Fairfax; at Wakefield in '45, he had captured a detachment of Cavalier soldiers in the shadow of Sandal Castle.

Oates' cousin Joshua Greathead, a gentleman of Gildersome, had also made his mark in the fight against the king's men. In February 1643 he had led a band of rebels to capture Howley Hall, the grand seat of Batley's Sir John Savile, and gone on to serve in the Roundheads' Bradford garrison.

These were the men who, as murmurs of rebellion grew louder throughout the North in the wake of the Restoration, plotted to bring the revolt to Farnley Wood – and to take the city of Leeds by storm.

The plot had been hatched that summer. With the connivance of local churchmen and minor nobles, Greathead and Oates had met several times with men such as Jeremiah Marsden, a radical minister, and Captain Robert Atkinson of Mallerstang. It was agreed that Atkinson, a career soldier, would mount a rebellion in Westmorland – modern-day Cumbria – in support of that spearheaded by Oates and Greathead at Farnley Wood.

But it seemed the gods were not on their side. As autumn gave way to winter, the weather worsened. Oates and Greathead bickered over the timing of the revolt.

WHO WERE THE FARNLEY WOOD PLOTTERS?

The renegades who gathered at Farnley Wood under Greathead and Oates were local men. Many of them were former soldiers, their rebellious spirit forged amid the blood and thunder of the Civil War.

John Taylor of Bingley had served under the regicide Captain Lilburne, a Cromwellian who had signed the death warrant of King Charles I. Sam Ellis, a veteran of Adwalton Moor, arrived at the rendezvous bearing two military trumpets. Richard Oldroyd, 'the Devil of Dewsbury', had been a trooper.

Ex-corporal Joseph Crowther, of Morley, brought with him 500 bullets, and, filling his blunderbuss, pledged bleakly that he would 'bring some of them down'. These were tough men, and they meant business.

Others, however, missed out. One Henry Rowntree refused to join the rising, causing his wife to weep in disappointment; Leeds man William Applegarth, on the other hand, said that he *would* have joined up, 'but was afraid it would too much discontent his mother'.

These were, perhaps, the lucky ones.

By 12 October – the night the conspirators had chosen to stage their coup – the rain was falling in torrents, waters ran high throughout the North and one commentator warned of 'great floods'.

On the bleak heights of Kaber Rigg in Westmorland, Captain Atkinson and his rabble of supporters were dismayed to find that the reinforcements they had expected had not arrived; planned rebellions in Durham and Northallerton, too, melted away in the teeth of the storms.

But at Farnley Wood the rebels were mustering. They, at least, would play their hand as best they could.

Altogether, they were thirty. Oates, carrying a case of pistols and an unsheathed rapier, was foremost. Most were mounted; all were well armed. What was more, they, unlike Atkinson, had reinforcements: more armed rebels were marching to meet them from

Leeds, Holbeck and Bradford. There were also rumours of planned uprisings in Holmfirth and Dewsbury.

But before long, as no support materialised, Oates, deep in the rainy wood, realised that the game was up. He disbanded his men – better, he thought, to let them live to fight another day than to risk their lives in a hopeless cause. The despondent rebels headed home.

Most of them would not see the spring.

The Farnley Wood revolt had been betrayed – by its own leader. Joshua Greathead, Captain Oates' co-conspirator, had turned informer in the early summer. He was not the only one. The whole region was riddled with spies in the pay of Yorkshire High Sheriff Sir Thomas Gower. The 'conspiracy' had been blown wide open.

The betrayals continued as the rebels were rounded up. Several gave evidence against their fellows in order

Left *Clifford's Tower in 1644, where the plotters were held.* (THP)

Right *The now demolished Moot Hall. The heads of the Farnley Plotters remained on display here for years.* (THP)

to save their own skins – Ralph Oates, the captain's son, among them. Others escaped the worst punishment by virtue of their social position: the clergymen in the plot, for example, all escaped with their lives.

In January 1664 the executions began.

Captain Oates was among the first to die, one of sixteen executed at York on 16 January. Three more were executed at Chapel Allerton three days later: their severed heads were displayed on spikes at Moothall End (on Briggate), where they would remain, mouldered and flyblown, until 1677. The

28 March saw three further executions at Abbleby, in Westmorland; Oldroyd, the 'Devil of Dewsbury', was executed in July, and Captain Robert Atkinson in September.

In total, twenty-four men paid the ultimate price for their part in the plot.

The treacherous Joshua Greathead, of whom it was truly said by a contemporary that 'it was a very dangerous thing to be in his company', was rewarded with a lucrative post as a tax collector. He ended his life in a London debtor's prison – and it is said that his loathsome ghost still haunts the town of Gildersome.

AD 1678

THE KILLING OF
LEONARD SCURR

IN A POOR TOWN, a hard town, a workers' town, a man with money might be well-advised to keep the information to himself. Otherwise, he lays himself open to resentment, envy – and worse.

Beeston, in the mining heartland of south Leeds, was once such a town. Leonard Scurr was a man with money. 'Worse' pretty much covers the fate that befell Leonard Scurr.

Scurr had served as a minister in Beeston during the 'protectorate' of Oliver Cromwell. His reputation was ambiguous. On the one hand, he was a good and diligent minister, a 'constant godly preacher'. On the other, he had a knack for getting into arguments. He had a keen legal mind, and a passion for bringing lawsuits – lawsuits that in the end only brought him debt, and trouble, and ultimately drove him out of his ministry.

Scurr did not leave his troubles behind him when he left the Church. In 1663, he was arrested on suspicion of playing a part in the treasonous Farnley Wood Plot. Some even sought to have him excommunicated.

The year 1678 found Leonard Scurr living with his mother and working

as a colliery manager. This was how he came by the substantial sum of money that would, in the end, spell his doom. The money was trading capital; Scurr planned to take it with him on a forthcoming business trip to London.

Word travels fast in a small town.

On a bleak January night in 1679 – the night before Scurr was to travel south – the door of the little house Scurr shared with his mother and a maidservant was broken open. In surged a mob, hell-bent on robbery and murder.

Mrs Scurr was seized first. At the sound of her screams, Scurr, who had been sleeping, leapt from his bed and hurtled downstairs – rapier in hand. Scurr was not a young man, but he was brave, and quick, and skilful. Two of the robbers fell to the blade of his rapier. A third, lunging savagely with an axe, struck Scurr's arm, severing his hand – and yet he fought on.

Scurr, blocking and slashing, battled his way to a trapdoor in the floor of the house that represented his only hope of escape. But the robbers had got there first. The trapdoor was locked. Valiant Leonard Scurr, backed into a corner, fought as long and as hard as he could

– but at length he fell, murdered by the mob. His mother, too, was killed in cold blood.

The third occupant of the house, the servant girl, pleaded with the robbers to spare her life. They would, perhaps, have shown mercy – had it not been for the influence of one member of the gang, a woman, who urged her comrades on to further cruelties. At her instigation, the servant girl was beheaded at the door of the house. Then the house was stripped of its contents, and set on fire. The mob fled.

And that would have been the end of it – nothing left but the charred ruin of a house amid the bleak Beeston pit-heads – had the gang's ringleader known when to keep his mouth shut.

His name was Holroyd. In the aftermath of the triple murder, he had fled to Ireland, taking his mistress with him. There, the pair had fallen into conversation with a young woman named Phoebe. By a striking coincidence, Phoebe had once worked as a servant girl for Leonard Scurr and his mother; Holroyd, with staggering indiscretion, proceeded to discuss the circumstances of the Scurrs' sad death. We don't know what yarn he spun. Whatever it was, it wasn't enough to hide the fact that his mistress, sitting beside him as he talked, was wearing Mrs Scurr's cloak, and Mrs Scurr's red petticoat.

Phoebe alerted a magistrate, and Holroyd was apprehended. Another member of the gang, one Littlewood, was also hauled in. The pair were tried and convicted in 1682. Littlewood was not given the death sentence, in the hope that he would provide further

Ralph Thoresby rode to the house on the day the crime was discovered, 'to see the most dreadful spectacle that was ever beheld in these parts':

Mr Scurr, his mother, and a maid servant, every one was burnt to death ... The old gentlewoman was the most burnt; her face, legs, and feet, were quite consumed to ashes, the trunk of her body much burnt, her heart hanging as a coal out of the midst of it. Part of his face and arms, with the whole body, unburnt, but as black as coals, his hands and feet quite consumed. Very little of the maid was to be found, only I saw her head; a most piteous sight! Some observe all their skulls broken, as it were, in the same place, which causes some to suspect it is wilfully done; but if so, the Lord will reveal it, so that, in all probability, these inhuman murderers may have their deserts in this life.

Ralph Thoresby, who visited the crime scene. (THP)

A GRAND DAY OUT?

When the murderous Holroyd went to the gallows, a crowd of 30,000 turned out at Holbeck Moor to see him hang. Public executions were an immensely popular form of entertainment; Holroyd was far from the only Leeds sinner to have his neck stretched in front of an appreciative audience.

THE WITCH OF LEDSTON

In 1593, the village of Ledston, in the far east of the borough of Leeds, was shaken by the death of one William Witham. Witham, the villagers said, had surely been bewitched to death. Ten years later, the 'witch', local woman Mary Pannel, was arrested, tried and put to death on a Ledston hill – a place now known as Mary Pannel Hill.

ATKINSON, THE BOY KILLER

Robert Atkinson of Whitkirk, Leeds, was only fifteen when in 1806 he murdered a girl named Elizabeth Stocken by striking her in the head with the claw-end of a hammer. Despite his tender years, the 'depraved youth' was sentenced to hang. His execution, like those of many Leeds villains, took place not in Leeds but in York – the hanging capital of the North.

BROWN THE POISONER

The people of Leeds knew Joe Brown first as a 'holy man', then as a deaf-and-dumb fortune-teller – and then, finally, as a murderer. Brown and an accomplice adopted the 'fortune-teller' disguise (Brown as the mute prophet, the accomplice as his interpreter) as a cover for their prolific career as thieves and burglars. In 1809, faced with transportation to Australia, Brown confessed to poisoning his landlady. He swung for it in October.

information about the gang that butchered the Scurrs. Holroyd, however, cold and unrepentant to the last, was hanged.

Despositions of the Castle of York reports Thoresby's version of the day's events. Holroyd stopped at the vicarage at Leeds on his way to the gallows, where he perished in 'the most resolute manner that eye ever beheld, wishing (upon the top of the ladder) he might never come where God had anything to do if he was guilty, and so threw himself off in an anger as it were, without any recommendation of himself to God that any could observe, which struck tears into my eyes, and terror to my heart, for his poor soul.'

AD 1795

THE BLACK RIVER RISES

THE DARK WATER of the River Aire has always been the lifeblood of Leeds. Even when it was choked with effluent, so fouled by industry that no fish or insects could live in it, the Aire was the city's sustaining artery. Without it, there would never have been a city here – Leeds would never have existed.

Sometimes, however, the river, in return for the wealth that it has brought to the city built on its banks, seems to demand sacrifices – and the city has no choice but to meet its terrible price.

The winter of 1794-5 was severe and long-lasting. The Aire froze solid. Snow settled thickly in the streets. Of course, for the people of Leeds, these things were nothing new – back then, winters *were* winters. It wasn't the Big Freeze they were afraid of; it was the Big Thaw.

The *Leeds Intelligencer* suggested fearfully that the fierce frosts and heavy snow might 'portend a great swell in the rivers' once the winter relaxed its grip. And so, indeed, they did.

Shortly after midnight on 9 February, the riverside folk who worked on the 'tenters' – the timber frames on which milled cloth was hung to dry – were awoken by a terrible noise from the snow-covered Aire. The mercury had inched its way just far enough up the thermometer; the thaw had come. With a roaring, creaking groan, the frozen river was breaking apart.

The tenter folk had just enough time to scramble, freezing and disoriented, from their beds, and flee for their lives, before the floods struck.

A freezing wall of water and ice came roaring down the riverway shortly before dawn. Tenters were smashed apart. Houses and dye-works were demolished. Above Leeds Bridge, a boat was torn from its moorings and smashed into pieces. Great bergs of ice slammed into the bridge's supports and wedged beneath its arches, blocking the current; the swollen Aire broke its banks, pouring in a black torrent into Meadow Lane and Hunslet Lane. The floodwaters rose higher here than ever before.

At the riverside, two more vessels were caught up in the maelstrom, ripped from their moorings and flung ashore further down the river's course. The icy water roared through the basements and lower floors of the riverside warehouses; carts, furniture and other cargo were stolen

THE MURDEROUS RIVER AIRE

The Aire is one of England's great rivers, flowing 70 miles from the Yorkshire Dales to the North Sea. Many further times it would rise up and wreak havoc...

1765

One Mr Smith, seeing a young boy swept up in the flooding Aire, dived some 20ft from a bridge to save the child. He succeeded. Tragically, 100 years later, his great-great nephew Lyndon Smith was drowned trying to rescue a girl who, while skating, had plunged through the ice on Benyon's Pond, Gledhow.

1775

A wild October flood overwhelmed the Water Lane district, inundating the streets to a depth of 7ft. The bridges at Calverley and Swillington were wrecked. But there was one lucky escapee: a hare, which survived the flood by riding to safety on top of the floating body of a drowned sheep.

1824

A Mr Brontë was among those horrified when, at Crow Hill, above Haworth, a swath of boggy moorland ruptured, sending a torrent of water, mud and peat thundering down the glen and into the Aire. Several children in the hamlet of Pondens were only barely snatched to safety. The waters of the Aire were so fouled by the discharge that for several days they could not be cooked with, drunk or even used in industry.

The 'black' River Aire. (Russell James Smith)

away by the rampaging flood. The bodies of drowned horses bobbed in the water.

And, somewhere, for some reason, five men in a Leeds ale-house decided that this was the perfect time for a spot of pleasure-boating. The five – 'too warm with liquor, and determined on a frolick', as the *Intelligencer* put it – commandeered a boat and cast off, the current at once whisking their flimsy craft away into the midst of the roaring, berg-strewn Aire.

It was, of course, only a matter of time.

They made it over one weir, the speed of their uncontrolled descent carrying them clear of the rapids. At this point, it might still all have seemed like a terrific lark; or perhaps, by now, a terrible clarity was setting in among the five drunken sailors – perhaps, as they hurtled toward the foaming Hunslet dam, they were sober enough to see that now, surely, their fun was about to come to an abrupt end.

As they mounted to the weir, clinging for dear life to their flood-tossed vessel, the inevitable happened: the boat spun, turning side-on to the current. It hit the weir. Over it went.

The five were pitched into the freezing river. Each struck out desperately for shore. Three of them made it. As they waited for their comrades to join them shivering on the riverbank, sobriety must have begun to quickly set in – and it must quickly have turned to despair as they watched the black waters rushing by, and gradually, numbingly, realised that their friends were lost to the pitiless river.

AD 1809

THE YORKSHIRE WITCH

IN 1796, a fire broke out at Marshall and Benyon's linen factory on Water Lane, Holbeck. It soon raged out of control. Amid the flames, a wall collapsed; seven people were killed, and twenty were wounded. For the people of industrial Holbeck, it was a tragedy. For Mary Bateman, the Yorkshire Witch, it was an opportunity.

Mary was twenty-eight. Born Mary Harker in Asenby, North Yorkshire, she had moved to York to work as a dressmaker in 1788 – and shortly thereafter been forced to flee to Leeds to avoid charges of theft.

There's little doubt that the charges were well-founded.

In Leeds, she established a dual career as both a mantua-maker and a 'wise woman', purporting to tell fortunes and remove curses. Soon she caught the eye of local wheelwright John Bateman; the pair were married in 1792, after a courtship that lasted just three weeks.

The Batemans made their home on High Court Lane in the Calls district of Leeds. John made wheels; Mary made mantuas, peddled 'witchcraft', and maintained a profitable sideline in petty theft.

As a thief, Mary was more prolific than skilful. More than once she was caught stealing money from her neighbours (and even her own lodgers). Usually she managed to avert scandal by paying off her victims. She had no scruples, either, about swindling her unfortunate husband: on at least one occasion, having duped him into leaving town, she promptly sold all of his clothes and furniture.

Mary Bateman, the Yorkshire Witch. (THP)

In the aftermath of the 1796 fire, Mary's keen instinct for con-trickery kicked in in earnest. Her first call was at the home of Miss Maude, a Leeds lady known for her tender heart and charitable ways. Among the dead, Mary lamented, had been the child of a poor woman, who had no linen on which to lay out the child's body. Could Miss Maude, for pity's sake, find it in her heart to donate a pair of sheets?

Miss Maude could indeed. Mary's next stop was the local pawnbroker's.

Mary repeated this brazen scam at least three times. And she wasn't finished yet. Now posing as a nurse from Leeds General Infirmary, she toured the district collecting linen 'to dress the wounds of those injured in the fire'. Needless to say, none of it went to the hospital; all of it went to Uncle.

Perhaps this was the last straw for John Bateman. He had never been party to any of Mary's schemes and frauds, but he must surely have been aware that his bold wife was gathering something of a reputation. In any case, it was shortly after the fire that John joined the army – taking 'his plague', as one biographer put it, with him. But Mary would not be gone for long.

By 1806 the Batemans were back in Leeds and Mary was up to her old tricks. She had inveigled herself into a community of local 'Southcottians'. These were followers of the visionary, pamphleteer and so-called prophet Joanna Southcott. One of Southcott's distinctive protocols was a process of 'sealing', in which a circle was drawn on a piece of paper and a message of acceptance written within; the follower signed at the top, and Southcott, after signing at the bottom, applied to the folded paper her own personal seal (a drawing of two stars and the letters IC, for *Iesu Christi*).

It was a simple-minded process that was ripe for exploitation by a canny operator like Mary. Having got her hands on a Southcott seal, she proceeded to present to the Southcottians of Leeds an astonishing miracle: her blessed hen, by the grace of God, had laid three eggs, each bearing the inscription 'Christ is Coming'. The gullible gathered to see; Mary charged them a shilling apiece.

Not too much imagination is required to see how Mary's 'miracle' had been effected. To her list of crimes could now be added that of eye-watering cruelty to a hen.

It was around this time, with Mary approaching the age of forty, that her offences took an even darker turn. Always skilled at manipulating the credulous in her guise as a 'wise woman', Mary now began to turn the screw.

A Mrs Greenwood was told that her husband, who was out of town, had been arrested on a serious charge and that he would be dead by morning unless four pieces of gold (plus a few trinkets thrown in for verisimilitude) were handed over to Mary. Mrs Greenwood protested that she had no gold; Mary suggested that she steal some.

Barzillai Stead, a failed businessman, was worked up by Mary to such a pitch of paranoia that – rather than face the bailiffs who, Mary assured him, were closing in on him – he joined the army, and handed over his enlistment fee to Mary. His wife, at the same time, was persuaded that Barzillai would surely elope with his 'mistress' unless Mary was given three half-crowns (the demand, of course, was leavened with a mix of mystical hokum). Once poor Barzillai – who had no mistress – was gone to his regiment, Mary Bateman proceeded to skin his wife to the bone.

A young relation of Mrs Stead's who had fallen pregnant, meanwhile, was talked into paying Mary for a series of 'charms' that would entice her baby's father – and then, when that failed, the eligible son of a family for whom the girl worked in service – to marry her. When no proposal was forthcoming, Mary then sold her medicines that effected an abortion, and wrecked the girl's health.

It was potent medicines of this sort that would prove the undoing of the Yorkshire Witch. Fortune-telling and 'wise woman' mumbo-jumbo might have been unethical, but it was unlikely to land Mary in court; poisoning was another matter entirely.

Whispers of poisoning surrounded Mary for years. In 1803, the Kitchin sisters, both old friends of Mary's, fell ill. Mary tended to them in their sickness. Nevertheless, they weakened rapidly; what was more, their mother, visiting from Wakefield, began to show symptoms of the same malady. All three died within days of each other. The official diagnosis was cholera; a local doctor swore they had been poisoned; Mary said that it was the plague. Mary's verdict was the one that caught the popular imagination: for days after the deaths, no one dared to venture near the 'plague-ridden' Kitchin house. More than enough time for Mary to plunder almost all of the family's belongings.

Mary's unlikely nemesis was a Bramley clothier named William Perigo. Perigo's wife, Rebecca, was suffering from pains in her chest; a local quack had told her that the ailment was caused by an 'evil wish'. Rebecca's niece had heard of a 'wise woman' in Leeds who had the power to lift such curses. Mary Bateman was duly sent for.

One of Mary's favourite tricks in running scams such as this was to invent another, fictional 'wise woman' to whom could be attributed incredible powers and unearthly authority. In the past she had often used a 'Mrs Moore'; with the Perigos, she claimed that the healing would be done by a 'Miss Blythe' in Scarborough.

Mary proceeded to, as one historian put it, 'excite their hopes then rouse their fears, all the time draining their purse'.

'Miss Blythe' sent numerous letters of instruction; she always ordered that they be destroyed, and promised that terrible things would befall the Perigos if they ever disclosed the secrets they contained.

In return, Mary – acting, of course, as Miss Blythe's representative – obtained from the Perigos a staggering quantity of goods. In just five months she had relieved the family of two pairs of men's shoes, several shirts, a counterpane, a silk handkerchief, a silk shawl, a skirt, a cotton gown, two pillowslips, a new waistcoat, 60lb of butter, quantities of meal, malt, tea and sugar, 200 or 300 eggs, two pairs of stockings, three bottles of spirits, two barrels, a piece of beef, and a goose.

Then, in May 1808, Mary told the Perigos that she had received from Miss Blythe a recipe for a curative 'honey and powder' mixture. She proceeded to systematically feed the powder to Rebecca in a pudding. The extraordinarily trusting Rebecca also dutifully swallowed seven spoonfuls of Miss Blythe's honey.

THE WITCH'S GHOULISH LEGACY

———∞———

Leeds Royal Infirmary charged the sensation-seekers of Leeds threepence each for a look at the body of the Yorkshire Witch. They flocked to see her, as the Southcottians had flocked to see her miraculous eggs: the hospital raised more than £30, and it wasn't finished with her yet.

The renowned William Hey conducted a public dissection of her body, raising some £80. Mary's skin was tanned and given away to superstitious applicants.

Finally, her tongue was preserved, in a curious nod to folkloric beliefs regarding the magical properties of a witch's tongue. It was displayed at Bolling Hall Museum until the 1950s, when it began to moulder, and at last was thrown away.

Leeds had wrung every drop of value it could from the body of Mary Bateman. It was not, perhaps, an ill-fitting fate.

Her tongue swelled horribly. Her mouth turned black. She was dead before the month's end.

The doctor Thomas Chorley had been summoned by William Perigo, but he had arrived too late to save Rebecca. Suspicious of Miss Blythe's 'powder', Chorley made a pudding from the substance and fed it to a cat. The cat died. The net was closing on Mary Bateman.

Astonishingly, there was still time for the Yorkshire Witch to launch a final assault on the grieving Mr Perigo. Having suffered illness himself from eating a small portion of the 'powder and honey', Perigo had been sent to Buxton to recuperate. Mary Bateman was waiting for him when he returned.

But the clothier was, by now, wise to her heartless scheme. One of Mary's 'spells' had involved sewing pouches filled with guinea notes – the Perigos' guinea notes, of course – into Rebecca's mattress. After his wife's death, Perigo had opened the pouches. They contained nothing but waste paper.

Perigo took two witnesses with him to confront Mary on the bank of the Leeds-Liverpool Canal. This didn't stop Mary from accusing Perigo of poisoning her – but this time no one listened to her lies. She was arrested for fraud. After being questioned by magistrates, she was charged with the wilful murder of Rebecca Perigo.

In March 1809, Mary stood trial. Dr Thomas Chorley testified that a bottle found in Mary's possession contained rum, oatmeal and arsenic. Her guilt was clear. Mary was sure to hang. But her resourcefulness had not yet been exhausted.

In a last-ditch bid to dodge the gallows, Mary declared that she was twenty weeks pregnant. A jury of married women was hastily assembled to test the truth of this claim; it did not take them long to find it to be false.

The judge sentenced her to be hanged from the neck until she was dead; ordered that her body be given to surgeons to be dissected and anatomised; and asked Almighty God to have mercy on her soul.

She was hanged on 20 March 1809.

AD 1826

INVASION OF THE BODY-SNATCHERS

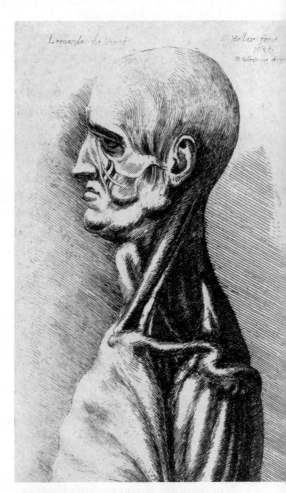

BODY-SNATCHING HAS A long and not-entirely-ignoble history. In the sixteenth century, for instance, the great Italian physician Vesalius stole executed corpses from the gibbet to pursue his studies in anatomy. Leonardo da Vinci had done the same. In fact, Italian medical students were getting into trouble for pilfering the dead as far back as 1319.

But in Britain the taboo surrounding the practice was far worse. It was no good pointing out that the corpses were being used for the helpful purpose of dissection – if anything, that only made things worse, as it was widely believed that being picked apart in the anatomy theatre imperilled one's prospects in the Eternal Life to come. It was literally seen to be a fate worse than death. 'I am certain of being hanged,' lamented Smithfield butcher and murderer Vincent Davis in 1725, 'but for God's sake, don't let me be anatomised!'

For centuries, only executed felons could legally be dissected. In Scotland in 1506, the Guild of Surgeons and Barbers was given an annual allowance of 'ane condampnit man after he be deid to mak anatomea of'; in England some

Studies like this were vital to the advancement of medical science. (With kind permission of the Thomas Fisher Rare Book Library, University of Toronto)

forty years later, Henry VIII granted the bodies of 'foure persons condempned, adjudged, and put to death for feloni' to the Company of Barber-Surgeons. This annual allowance crept up by only the merest increments: in 1565, Elizabeth I offered four dead malefactors to the Company of Physicians; in 1663, the surgeons' quota was upped to six by Charles II.

With the science of surgery booming in the mid-to-late 1700s, medical schools faced a chronic shortage of cadavers. Even those that they were legally allowed they had to fight for: theatres of execution, such as Tyburn in London, were regularly the scene of pitched battles as the friends and families of those executed fought to prevent their loved ones' earthly remains from being carted off by the beadles of the surgical companies.

There's little doubt that most if not all of the great surgeons of the eighteenth century were driven to dabble, at least to some extent, in the dark arts of the body-snatchers – the shadowy, dirty-fingernailed men who, with grim gallows humour, were dubbed 'the Resurrectionists'.

Scotland was perhaps the spiritual home of this grimy brotherhood. With Glasgow and Edinburgh supporting thriving medical schools, body-snatchers had been busy in the graveyards there for decades: as early as 1711, there had been reports of 'a violation of sepulchres in the Grey-Friars Churchyard'. While in Glasgow medical students were usually forced to do their own body-snatching, the learned professors of Edinburgh usually preferred to subcontract the work to the 'sack-'em-up men'.

The body-snatchers hunted in packs, and walked a legal knife-edge. It was thought that, because a corpse belonged to no one, stealing one was no crime; the theft of a grave-shroud, a coffin or a wedding-ring, however, could be a capital offence.

Often, and in spite of widespread public disgust, the courts took a lenient stance. Those in power understood that skilled surgeons were needed, not least to slice and stitch the men of the country's army and navy. Even if an unlucky Resurrectionist was fined or sentenced to prison, it was likely that one or more of his high-society clients would bail him out. The surgeons themselves were hardly ever prosecuted for their part in fuelling the thriving black market in corpses.

And they could be remarkably open about the practice.

In 1828, addressing a Parliamentary Select Committee, surgeon Sir Astley Cooper chillingly told the assembled MPs that 'the law does not prevent our obtaining the body of an individual if we think proper'. 'There is no person,' he added, possibly with a glitter in his eye, 'let his situation in life be what it may, whom, if I were disposed to dissect, I could not obtain.'

Leeds' first brush with the body-snatching menace occurred in the winter of 1826. Winter was the Resurrectionists' busy time; once the weather warmed up, corpses began to rot too quickly and anatomy schools suspended their lectures. The gang in this case was led by George Cox and Michael Armstrong. Cox was the son of a box-maker; his own talents, evidently, were more in the way of box-breaking.

Sir Astley Cooper. (NARA, 525430)

The first was Mr Daniel. He'd been buried in St John's churchyard on New Year's Day, but his grave had been found broken open and empty. The Resurrectionists had managed to spirit his body out of the city, but they didn't quite manage to move it on; it was discovered, neatly boxed, at a post-station in Newcastle, *en route* to a 'Mr Simpson' in – where else? – Edinburgh.

The coach-office clerk identified George Cox as the man who had despatched the package. Cox claimed that the box had been prepared by 'a stranger Jew' who had been lodging with his family, and that he'd had no knowledge of its grisly contents. It didn't wash. He got six months in York Castle. And yet the body-snatching went on.

Mary Oddy, the fifteen-year-old daughter of an Armley family, was next to be dragged from her grave and offered for sale by the gang. Children – known in the trade as 'smalls' – were priced by the inch. In February, the corpse of a sixty-year-old man was intercepted, again at Newcastle, again on its way to a buyer in Edinburgh. The vast number of cadavers that must have been travelling undetected along the country's coachways during this period is one of the most unsettling aspects of the Resurrectionists' boom years.

They nailed Michael Armstrong in March; he, too, got six months at York.

With the notorious sack-'em-up gang in prison, Leeds' body-snatching panic subsided. Now, perhaps, the city's dead could rest peacefully in their graves. But they would not do so for long. The Resurrection Men would be back.

AD 1831

THE RESURRECTIONISTS' RETURN

TOM ROTHERY, a dyer of Leeds, led an unexceptional life. His death in 1831, while horrible (he was fatally scalded after falling into a vat of boiling dye), was not particularly unusual at the time. But *after* his death, he found himself caught up in a remarkable adventure – thanks to John Hodgson, Leeds' most notorious body-snatcher.

John Hodgson was not a surgeon – he wasn't even a medical student. He was a clerk to a Mr Gaunt, a Leeds attorney.

On the last day of May in 1831– rather late in the season for the Resurrectionists – a Leeds coachman reported that three young men had hired him to take them, and their large carpet-bag, to a churchyard in Wortley, south Leeds. On arrival, one of the men instructed him to drive his carriage into a field near to the coachyard, out of sight of passers-by, and wait there while the three went about their business.

When they returned a short while later, their carpet-bag was full.

The coachman reported that, on the journey back into the city, the men talked with satisfaction of having acquired a 'subject'. Then they bickered about where to take their unwieldy cargo. Eventually they came to a decision: the coachman was ordered to drop them at the offices of the attorney Mr Gaunt.

It was here, not long afterwards, that the decomposing corpse of the dyer Tom Rothery was found, locked in a box in a lumber-hole beneath the staircase. A sign tacked to it read 'Books: please to keep dry'.

The hunt for the dyer's body had begun when Rothery's grave had been found open and the coffin broken into. A reward of £5 had immediately been offered for the body's return. The coachman had led the police to Gaunt's office – and to Gaunt's clerk, the hard-working, intelligent and 'very respectable' John Hodgson.

Hodgson's immediate response to his exposure was to flee to Harrogate. But he was apprehended and returned to Leeds for trial. In court, he mounted a defence not only of his own actions but of the practice of dissection in general.

He had, it transpired, spent time studying in Edinburgh, that hotbed of surgeons and sack-'em-up men. Mention of the city in this context was surely enough to raise a shudder in the

The execution of William Burke. (THP)

'It is nature,' he said, 'that teaches us to use the bodies of the dead to preserve the bodies of the living.'

The prosecutor, Mr Blackburne, agreed that a surgeon's need for dissection subjects might constitute a 'palliation' in a case of body-snatching – but 'surely it was only a palliation to those who were in that profession to which mankind owed so much, and to whom it was necessary for the benefit of science and to enable men to assist their fellow creatures'.

In response, Hodgson pointed out that it was not possible to become a surgeon without first learning anatomy – and how was that to be done without cadavers to study?

Leeds' surgical establishment was not untouched by the sensational trial. Hodgson confessed that he had been 'connected with a medical man in the taking of this body'; it had been their intention to dissect Rothery's corpse together.

'I could not give up his name,' he added, 'without utterly ruining him.'

courtroom: memories were still fresh of the trial and execution in 1829 of the murderer William Burke, who with his partner William Hare had murdered at least fifteen people in Edinburgh – in order to sell their corpses to the city's surgeons.

Hodgson addressed the court in a voice so hushed that reporters from the local press struggled to hear him. The dissection of corpses had a noble history, he argued; it was only in 'modern times' that the practice had become taboo.

Leeds Medical School. An unnamed doctor from this establishment may have been training would-be doctor and body-snatcher Hodgson using stolen corpses. (THP)

SCHOOL FOR SAWBONES

In 1831, seven surgeons of Leeds convened to create a School of Medicine 'for the purposes of giving such courses of lectures on subjects connected with Medicine and Surgery as will qualify for examination at the College of Surgeons and Apothecaries' Hall'.

There was, of course, already an impressive surgical tradition in the city. The great William Hey had founded Leeds' General Infirmary in 1767, and served as its chief surgeon until his retirement in 1812. Pudsey-born Hey was a major figure in British surgery's first golden – if gruesome – age. The pioneering scientist Joseph Priestley – the man who discovered oxygen – described him as 'the only person in Leeds who gave any attention to my experiments'. His influence lives on in the names of the many medical conditions in which he specialised, including Hey's Encysted Hernia and Hey's Internal Derangement of the Knee. He was a popular and skilled lecturer, regularly dissecting the corpses of executed criminals before audiences of gawping students.

Hey's grandson, **William Hey III**, was one of the seven remarkable surgeons who founded the Leeds School of Medicine.

Thomas Pridgin Teale, who gave the School's first-ever lecture, was another scion of a medical dynasty. Teale was among the first surgeons to encourage team-work in the operating theatre; he was also an early advocate of antiseptics, and a specialist in the surgical treatment of scrofulous neck and bladder-stones (a procedure of staggering unpleasantness).

Briggate-born **Charles Thackrah**, meanwhile, had been doctor to the city's poor since 1817. A sickly, TB-ravaged man, he nevertheless managed to attract the opprobrium of Leeds' Better Sort by fathering an illegitimate child after an affair with a patient. He also had a history of getting into scraps with his fellow surgeons.

A disagreement with William Hey over the coagulation of the blood – a dispute settled in Thackrah's favour by an experiment at a local slaughterhouse – was at least entirely professional; a later confrontation with senior surgeon **Samuel Smith** was less so, beginning with a fist-fight between one of Smith's apothecaries and one of Thackrah's students and petering out ignominiously when Smith challenged Thackrah to a public dissection contest (Thackrah wormed out of it by remarking snottily that one of his students might as well take his place).

The other three founders were **Joseph Garlick**, **Adam Hunter**, and **James Williamson**.

These men weren't in any sense squeamish: not about blood and guts, not about trampling on their colleagues' finer feelings, and certainly not about outraging narrow-minded public morality when it came to obtaining specimens – i.e. dead people – for dissection.

It's a pity that we'll never know which of them had John Hodgson on their payroll. Maybe none of them did. Maybe all of them did.

Perhaps Hodgson had heard tales of how the Edinburgh public had vilified Robert Knox, the surgeon who bought bodies from Burke and Hare. Sir Walter Scott had attacked him as a 'learned carcass-butcher'; a mob had gathered outside his home to strangle, hang and dismember an effigy of him.

In any case, the people of Leeds had their own suspicions about John Hodgson's likely customers. In the days following the body's discovery, Rothery's brother was arrested after confronting the surgeon Robert Baker and accusing him in no uncertain terms of being in cahoots with the body-snatcher. Baker, naturally, denied the charge – and later won an apology.

He was not the only surgeon to be caught up in the proceedings. Indeed, three of his colleagues appeared in court – supporting the young clerk's case.

William Wildsmith, a surgeon who specialised in treating the city's factory workers, testified that dissection was necessary if a person was to learn surgery. Thomas Thompson Metcalfe, an eccentric eye specialist fresh from a stint in Rothwell debtors' jail, told the court that Hodgson was a good anatomist and physiologist; a Dr Hirst endorsed his recommendation.

Concluding his defence, Hodgson issued a heartfelt and portentous plea: 'If you send me to prison,' he said, 'you will ruin my prospects in life for ever.'

The Deputy Recorder, presiding, took a sympathetic view of the young man's plight. He accepted that Hodgson had taken the body in order to dissect it himself, and not with the intention of selling it on. He wished, he said, perhaps wringing his hands as he spoke,

that some lawful and ethical means of supplying bodies for anatomising might be discovered...

But the bottom line was that it hadn't, and it was the court's 'bounden duty' to send John Hodgson to jail. Six weeks in York Castle.

We'll never know what might have happened if Hodgson had been permitted to continue in his covert surgical studies. Was his professed fascination with anatomy genuine, or a cynical bid to win the court's sympathy? Was he really an aspiring surgeon? Or was he a wannabe Resurrectionist all along?

All we know is that, if he didn't go into York Castle as a career sack-'em-up man, he certainly came out as one.

In November 1831, a suspicious package was found aboard a courier coach at the Rose & Crown Inn in central Leeds (where the Queen's Arcade now stands). The package had come from Manchester; it was addressed to 'Hon. Ben. Thompson, Mail Office, Edinboro: to be kept until called for'. It contained a young man's corpse.

At around the same time, another dubious parcel, addressed to 'Rev. Mr Geneste' in Selby, was intercepted *en route* from Manchester at the Bull & Mouth Hotel on Briggate. Officials noticed that it gave off a foul smell. On opening it, they discovered the dead bodies of a woman and a young girl.

The graverobbers' game was up.

Police investigations revealed that the man's body found at the Rose & Crown was that of Robert Hudson from the village of East Ardsley, between Leeds and Wakefield. Hudson had hanged himself in a coal-pit cabin a fortnight previously, and been buried at East

The Rose and Crown just before it was demolished. The body was hidden here. (By kind permission of the Leeds Library and Information Service)

Briggate, site of the Rose and Crown. The Rose and Crown was on the left, now the site of the Queen's Arcade. (THP)

Ardsley on 1 November. The village sexton confirmed that Hudson's grave was empty.

First to be hauled in by the police was butcher James Norman, who had been apprehended in the act of loading Robert Hudson's cadaver on to the mail carriage. Next, following a tip-off from the coachman, was schoolmaster John Pickering. When officers arrived at Pickering's house, they found him in conversation with a friend – one John Hodgson.

At Pickering's insistence, Hodgson accompanied Pickering into custody.

The investigation soon gathered momentum. On searching Pickering's rooms, police found a full Resurrectionist's toolkit: two mud-daubed spades, a sharp saw, a length of rope, a jemmy, a gimlet, and an outfit of muddied work clothes.

Then the police brought in one Henry Teale, a gentleman's servant, on suspicion of abetting the body-snatchers. They had found the gang's weak link. Teale told them everything.

John Hodgson, he said, was the ringleader. Teale had befriended the young clerk – who was still only twenty-two – at the annual Chapeltown Feast. They had gone drinking at the Blackwell Ox on Briggate, and arranged to meet up again. Soon Teale had won Hodgson's trust: Hodgson produced a list of churchyards, and told Teale that two bodies were needed.

On the night of 2 November, the gang assembled. In addition to Hodgson, Teale, Pickering and Norman, there were William Germain, a packer, John Wood, a shoemaker, William Bradley, a joiner, and Tom Pearson, a weaver. Two small carriages – 'gigs' – were ordered from a coach station on Trinity Street. The gang piled in. Their destination was the East Ardsley churchyard.

It was John Hodgson who searched the yard and gave the order to dig. The digging itself was Teale's job. When his spade struck a coffin lid, joiner Bradley took over, levering open the lid, heaving out the body (a 'small'), stripping it of its grave-clothes and bundling it into a sack. Teale filled in the grave.

Germain and Hodgson, meanwhile, were breaking open a second grave. Midway through, Hodgson, spooked by a sudden noise, whipped out two pistols: this was a man who meant business. The body they dragged from the broken coffin was larger than the first. It was a young man: the suicide Robert Hudson.

The gang drove the two corpses swiftly back to Leeds. They were unbagged in James Norman's shed in his father's yard on Woodhouse Lane. Germain and Bradley took charge of preparing them for postage: each was trussed, sewn into a canvas bag, and packed into a wooden box, which was sealed with strips of tin. The 'small' was quickly dispatched to its client – a surgeon in Edinburgh. Hudson's body, however, must have taken too long to box up. They missed the last coach. The body would have to stay in Norman's shed.

Over drinks in the Black Boy pub on Kirkgate, however, Norman made it plain that his father would not stand for the body being kept on his property. A somewhat half-baked Plan B was concocted: they would remove the body to Pickering's rented rooms on Tobacco Mill Lane, and from there transport it to the Rose & Crown coach-stop.

It was as Norman struggled to manhandle the body on to the coach that the police stepped in.

JOHN BISHOP.   WILLIAMS.   JAMES MAY.

Here was evidence not of mischief by medical students but of a nationwide traffic in stolen corpses. Clearly there were Resurrectionist trade routes between Leeds, Edinburgh and Manchester. Some even suggested that Hodgson had links with the 'London Burkers' (pictured above), a notorious body-snatching gang that ran wild in the capital from 1819 to 1831. At trial in that same winter of 1831, its leaders, John Bishop and Tom Williams, admitted to stealing and selling between 500 and 1,000 cadavers. Eventually they had gone too far: inspired by the Burke and Hare killings, they had turned to murder. Both were hanged at Newgate in December 1831.

In comparison, the Hodgson gang got off lightly. Teale, who had turned King's Evidence, walked free, as did the schoolmaster John Pickering. Bradley, Germain and Norman were all sentenced to three months' imprisonment. John Hodgson – attorney's clerk, aspiring surgeon, 'very respectable young man' and undisputed ringleader of the Leeds Resurrectionists – was sent down for a year.

AD 1832

KING CHOLERA STRIKES!

IT BEGAN IN SUNDERLAND, slum-ridden, smog-choked, some 80 miles to the north-east of Leeds. Who was the first? It may have been Robert Joyce, dead from a horrible sickness in the autumn of 1831; it may have been twelve-year-old Isabella Hazard, who, on a Sunday in October, fell ill after attending church and was dead within a day. The death on 23 October of Hazard's near neighbour, sixty-year-old shipworker William Sproat, confirmed the suspicions: cholera had arrived in England.

For many, the news was not as terrifying as it might have been (as, indeed, it *ought* to have been). The word 'cholera' was widely used in the nineteenth century to describe any illness that caused vomiting and diarrhoea – generally, this meant dysentery and food poisoning. After visiting the scene of the outbreak in Sunderland late in 1831, the Leeds doctor Charles Thackrah published a book recalling a 'cholera' epidemic in Leeds in 1825, which 'produced severe effects and considerable alarm'.

Thackrah surveyed the progress of the 1825 disease in Halton, Chapel Allerton, Kirkstall and inner Leeds. He also travelled to the south and west, to Wakefield (where the symptoms of an afflicted patient in the lunatic asylum included 'stools resembl[ing] cold oatmeal gruel'), Hanging Heaton, Batley, and the badly-affected town of Gawthorpe ('inhabited chiefly by weavers who, though not generally poor, are dirty in their persons and have their houses more than commonly filthy').

This 'English cholera' seems to have been grim indeed. Could the 'Spasmodic' or 'Malignant' cholera, newly arrived in Sunderland, possibly be any worse?

No, concluded Thackrah. It was true, he conceded, that the English cholera claimed far fewer lives than malignant cholera was known to have done in India, where it originated – but this was a consequence of the climate and food of that country, and the habits and character of the Indian people. It did not mean that the malignant cholera was a different disease.

'Could an Indian army, with its train of followers – enfeebled, debauched and fatigued, deficient in protection from the weather, deficient, especially, in nourishing food – have been encamped in England in 1825, we should have beheld, I conceive, the most appalling form of the disease,' Thackrah wrote.

The words have a sourly ironic ring. Enfeebled, fatigued, deficient in food and shelter: the description matches the poor labouring classes of Leeds' industry-soiled slums as well as any 'Indian army'.

But the important point is that Thackrah was simply wrong. Leeds had seen its share of disease, from bubonic plague through to typhus and tuberculosis. But it had never seen anything like the Cholera Morbus.

Prior to its appearance in Sunderland, physicians had tracked the progress of the disease across Asia and Europe. It had first been noticed among British troops in the Bengali town of Jessore. In 1823 it had reached Russia; press reports of the devastation wreaked in St Petersburg caused considerable unease among British health authorities.

In 1831, quarantine had been imposed on shipping from the infected Baltic ports: Hamburg, Riga, Danzig. But, at Sunderland, the quarantine had been breached. From there, the Cholera Morbus would spread through the cities of England like wildfire.

In Leeds, as elsewhere, it took only a small spark to trigger an outbreak.

The Dock family were Irish immigrants. They lived in Blue Bell Fold, a slummy cul-de-sac near Marsh Lane, just north of the Aire in the Bank district of the city. They made a meagre living as weavers.

Their son was two years old in the spring of 1832. On the morning of 26 May the boy was taken ill; at 5 o'clock that same afternoon, he died.

The next day, a child of the Docks' neighbours, the Tobins, was also struck down. In no time at all, twelve people in the district lay dead. The epidemic had taken hold.

Blue Bell Fold, site of a cholera outbreak. (By kind permission of the Leeds Library and Information Service)

Charles Thackrah described the gruesome symptoms of the Cholera Morbus. 'Ask the sufferer his first symptoms,' he wrote:

[and] he seems to know or recollect none. They have either been slight, or present agony has rendered him forgetful of past and minor pain.

Ask him what he suffers, he answers in a faint or broken voice, 'Oh my stomach! Oh the cramp!' Observe his countenance: it is darkly suffused. The eyes have an expression of indifference to external objects; the pupils are contracted, the vessels of the conjunctiva injected.

The tongue, ears and nose – indeed, the whole surface – is cold as a stone and more or less purple. The extremities are especially chilled; grasping the feet we feel a continued convulsive motion of the tendons. No pulse is to be found in any of the arteries and scarcely a beating even in the heart. The wretched man sometimes writhes with cramp and utters a cry; he is then still, and seems unconscious of surrounding objects.

After a time, perhaps, a faint attempt at reaction takes place: the skin is rather wanner and a clammy sweat breaks out; the cramps cease, but the heart and arteries soon give up the struggle. He sinks in a few hours, often without any other marked symptoms, and dies so placidly that the bystanders are not aware of his exit.

Further details come from a French doctor, François Boisseau, who in 1832 compiled a dossier of cholera symptoms observed as the disease swarmed westward through the Russian empire: 'Slight spasms were felt in the limbs, then dejections and vomiting of an aqueous matter mixed with whitish mucosities and sometimes worms were ejected from the stomach... the evacuations soon became violent... the cramps extended to the muscles of the abdomen and chest... the eyes became hollow, fixed and depressed in the orbits... thirst ardent, tongue red on its whole surface... excruciating pains and burning heat in the stomach and intestines.'

It was, it's clear, a truly horrible way to die.

The Cholera Morbus was as mysterious as it was awful. For one thing, no one knew how it spread. Most experts in contagion still believed that disease was associated with 'miasmas', or foul smells – and there was no shortage of those in industrial Leeds.

The bleak reality was that the disease spread not through the smell, but through the source of the smell: sewage. The accumulated filth of a city like Leeds was a breeding ground for the bacteria that caused cholera. The bacteria's lethal effects were triggered when a person drank water that was contaminated with sewage – and, for the poor, the water was pretty much always contaminated with sewage.

It's hard to overstate the foulness of Leeds' industrial slums in the early 1830s. Since the turn of the century, an uncontrollable population explosion had seen the number of people living in the city leap from around 53,000 to 123,000. Every nook, cranny and rat-hole in the town was occupied, maybe by a single worker, more often by a family (or several families). This posed obvious problems. Soon the city's streets – most unpaved and undrained – were slick with excrement and waste water. Rivers of raw sewage ran in the gutters.

Blue Bell Fold typified these conditions. The grim cul-de-sac stood by the bank of a stream carrying industrial effluent from the city's mills and dye-houses to the river. The river, according to a local journalist, was clogged with:

> the contents of about 200 water closets and similar places, a great number of common drains, the drainings from dunghills, the Infirmary (dead leeches, poultices for patients, etc), slaughter houses, chemical soap, gas, dung, dyehouses and manufactures, spent blue and black dye, pig manure, old urine wash, [and] all sorts of decomposed animal and vegetable substances.

There was little fresh air, little sunlight. Homes were cramped, and work – in the city's mills, dyeing plants or factories – was back-breaking.

These were, quite simply, cholera conditions.

The efforts that were made by the medical profession to ease the townspeople's suffering were on at least one occasion undermined by the townspeople themselves: when a Cholera Hospital was established at St Peter's Square, local homeowners – in an early manifestation of not-in-my-back-yard syndrome – rioted. The windows of the hospital were smashed; doctors and orderlies were harassed. A new site, on Saxton Lane, was hastily purchased.

More than 1,100 people were stricken with Cholera Morbus in Leeds during the '32 epidemic. Seven hundred died. The death toll was such that many victims' bodies went without a proper burial; one historian observed that some people – particularly 'individuals of the Roman Catholic persuasion' – made a habit of simply dumping a coffin in a churchyard, throwing a handful of dirt on its lid and then leaving it 'to take its chance'.

In 1833, Robert Baker, Thackrah's colleague at Leeds General Infirmary, conducted a landmark study of cholera cases across the city during the outbreak. His data was used by Edwin Chadwick in his best-seller *The Sanitary Condition of the Labouring Classes* (1842).

'By the inspection of the map of Leeds which Mr Baker has prepared at my request to show the localities of epidemic diseases,' Chadwick wrote, 'it will be perceived that they ... fall on the uncleansed and close streets and wards occupied by the labouring classes.'

'It will also be observed,' he added, 'that in the badly cleansed and badly drained wards ... the proportional mortality is nearly double that which prevails in the better conditioned districts.'

In other words, if you were poor, you were more likely to catch cholera, and, if you did catch cholera, you were more likely to die.

No wonder, with the epidemic at its height, the London journalist Henry Hetherington raged that 'the Cholera has arrived amongst us, and this, among other blessings, we have to lay at the door of our "glorious constitution" – for it is a disease begotten of that poverty and wretchedness which are occasioned by the wealth and luxury of the few to whom only the constitution belongs.'

Cholera Morbus would not easily be got rid of. After petering out in Leeds in the late summer of 1832, it returned to the city less than two years later. A more serious epidemic struck in 1849: again, the disease arrived from Europe via England's east-coast ports. Cholera cases aboard ships docked at Sunderland and Hull were soon followed by the news that it had spread inland, to Castleford. By June 1849, the disease was on the loose throughout the country.

Leeds again suffered severely. Again it was the Bank district that took the first blow: an Irishman named Mr McCarthey, of Wheeler Street, became the first victim of the '49 cholera on 12 June. Between June and October, when the epidemic finally burnt itself out, 1,674 people died either of cholera or of diarrhoea.

It isn't difficult to guess which areas were the worst hit. Again, the poor eastern quarters of the inner city bore the brunt: York Street, Marsh Lane, Quarry Hill, Newtown, Leylands and New Road End. Outer Leeds also had a hard time of it, Hunslet and Beeston in particular.

On 19 September, the Bishop of Ripon declared a 'day of humiliation' for the borough of Leeds. Shops and businesses would be closed at lunchtime so that people of the city would be free to attend special church services and pray, 'on account of the sore visitation with which it has pleased Almighty God to afflict it'. People were urged to 'beseech him of His great Mercy to stay the pestilence which is abroad'.

A special prayer was issued to churches throughout England; for the duration of the cholera epidemic, this

Leeds Infirmary. (THP)

was to replace the prayer usually said 'during any Time of Common Plague' – for the cholera was no common plague.

Another option was to put one's faith in quack medicines. Many did: the house of Captain Waterton, purveyor of a proprietary Cholera Powder, was reportedly besieged by anxious townspeople while the cholera was at its height.

More practical steps were taken by the city's surgeons. Desperate to root out the cause of the scourge, they adopted a rigorous hygiene policy: in the course of the epidemic, 868 beds, 258 pillows, 12 pillow cases, 375 coverlets, 546 blankets and 282 sheets were destroyed. All were later replaced at the city's expense. The zealous surgeons were not to know, of course, that in spite of their efforts the disease still lurked in the stinking gutters, filth-strewn streets and festering river-water.

These murderous outbreaks of cholera had a further damaging effect. In 1850, smallpox – at one time a mass killer, now largely under control thanks to Edward Jenner's discovery of a vaccine

– returned to Leeds. Understandably overwhelmed by the dreadful cholera epidemics, many people had neglected to get their children vaccinated.

Hunslet was struck by cholera again in 1854, when fifteen people – most of them employed at Wilkinson's flax mill, though naturally the mill-owners denied indignantly that their premises were to blame – died of the disease.

By this time the city's sanitary systems had improved – but not by much, and not for everyone. As late at 1870, only around 6,000 flushing toilets were in use in the whole of Leeds. The majority resorted to hole-in-the-floor privies, and 'middensteads' – that is, piles of human faeces – were still a common sight in the city streets. Indeed, one story told of a middenstead in Wellington Square 'which measures 21 feet long by 5 feet 10 inches broad, and which is 6 feet deep below the surface of the ground'.

'Into this middenstead,' the tale went on, 'there fell not long ago a half tipsy man, plunging deep into the revolting filth, and there, suffocated, he lay until, days afterwards, discovered by the scavengers.'

This was still a deeply dirty city. But the Cholera Morbus was gone – and has yet to return.

CHOLERA AND QUACKERY

No one knew how the terrible disease could be cured – how the scourge they called 'King Cholera' might be driven away.

We know now that cholera can be treated relatively easily, by replacing the natural liquids and salts that the body loses as a result of the exhausting disease. The doctors of the time had no such knowledge. Some (more by luck than judgment) did rehydrate their patients, and achieved good results; most persisted with quack treatments that could only make matters worse.

Leeds' Charles Thackrah, for instance, recommended bleeding with leeches, purging the bowel, and the administration of 'remedies' including brandy and ammonia, mustard flour, calomel (or mercurous chloride), chlorine, hydrochloruret of lime, tartarized antimony, nitrous oxide, 'galvanism' (electric shocks) and nitric acid. Other doctors prescribed tobacco enemas as a stimulant.

Ultimately, however, most had to fall back on the same conclusion as Thackrah: 'A reliance on the protection and providence of God enables us to meet with resolution the evils of life and often saves us from the worst.'

Cold comfort indeed for families such as the Docks.

AD 1835

HORROR IN HOLBECK

THE *ANNALS AND HISTORY of Leeds* described it as 'one of the most dreadful accidents that ever happened in the borough of Leeds'. The *Leeds Intelligencer* said that it was 'perhaps difficult to find a parallel in the annals of the northern counties'. The events of 28 October 1835 would, in every sense, shake the city of Leeds to its foundations.

The run-up to Guy Fawkes' Night on 5 November would have been a busy time for Holbeck firework-maker William Wood and his staff. On the evening of 28 October, at least one employee was working late at Wood's cottage: Susannah Dockray, one of several local girls who were paid a penny an hour by Wood to make 'squibs' and other fireworks.

Susannah worked by candlelight in an upstairs room in the Woods' family home. On this night, she had been twisting paper to make firecrackers. At the end of her shift, she went to snuff out her candle. The guttering candlewick loosed off a spark. Perhaps Susannah did not know, or had forgotten, that the room was crammed with gunpowder.

The law forbade manufacturers from storing more than 50lb of gunpowder in one place. Wood – perhaps anticipating a rush come the Guy Fawkes festivities – had stockpiled more than 130lb.

Across the road from the Woods' cottage, weaver Mr Walker, bent over his loom in an upstairs work-room, looked up to see sudden lights in the Woods' window: squibs, he saw, were shooting to and fro. Prudently, he took cover.

Meanwhile, Wood's wife Hannah was chatting in the family parlour with her daughter, also Hannah, and neighbour Mary Stephenson. Mary nursed her baby son, Joseph, as they talked.

A hissing, crackling sound from upstairs was the first sign the ladies had that something was amiss. Alarm soon turned to horror: footsteps clattered on the stairs, and into the room burst young Susannah Dockray, screaming in terror, and engulfed in flame.

Still ablaze, Susannah stumbled out of the house, followed by young Miss Wood and Mary Stephenson. Mrs Wood had also leapt to her feet – but she had no intention of fleeing. Her plan was bolder: she would grab the lit explosives and fling them from the window before they could destroy her family home and, with it, her family's livelihood. Despite Mary's cries of warning, she made for the stairs, yelling for water.

She didn't make it. She had barely reached the threshold of the room in which the explosives were housed before a barrel and a half of gunpowder exploded.

Exploding house in Holbeck! (THP)

The blast was heard as far afield as Armley, Kirkstall, Headingley and Chapeltown. At St Paul's church, more than a mile away in the centre of the city, congregants gathered for the evening service quailed in fear, believing, from the noise and juddering of the masonry, that their own church was giving way. The shockwave smashed windows and shattered equipment in mills and factories throughout Holbeck. The towering black chimney of Marshall's mill was seen to shake perceptibly.

Three houses were completely ruined by the blast: the Woods' cottage was levelled to the ground, and 'every article of furniture consumed by fire or crushed by timbers'. Mrs Wood, her daughter, and Mary Stephenson were all killed, as was baby Joseph Stephenson. Another neighbour, weaver's wife Mrs Walker, was also killed (the three others in the same house – including a three-year-old girl – escaped miraculously).

One Mr Stead, more than seventy years old and bed-bound, sustained horrible burns, and died soon afterwards.

An inquiry was hastily convened. The bodies of the dead were laid out for inspection. The report made distressing reading.

'All the three women were dreadfully crushed, particularly about the heads,' it was noted. 'Mary Stephenson's baby's skull was not merely flattened and broken into several pieces, but its head had been nearly severed from its body.'

Surgeon Robert Craven added grimly: 'The two Stephensons were very much mangled.'

The city of Leeds was left in shock. Perhaps some thought fearfully back to the appearance of Halley's Comet, a dark portent wherever it was seen, over the city only a fortnight before. And they would perhaps think of the explosion again when, a month later, the city was visited by the *aurora borealis*, and strange and ominous fire again lit up the Yorkshire sky.

Portent of evil: in 1066, as this image of the Bayeux Tapestry (from an Edwardian edition of Popular Science*) shows, Halley's Comet appeared before the Battle of Hastings, and was thought to portend 'a change in some kingdom'. In 1835 it could be seen before the disaster at Holbeck. (THP)*

AD 1837

FEARLESS FIREFIGHTERS

– or Drunk on Duty?

CHIEF CONSTABLE William Heywood was hailed as a hero in the immediate aftermath of the fierce fire that broke out in Water Lane, Leeds, in the summer of 1837. The area was central to the city's industry; it was the responsibility of the new Leeds Police Force to tackle it, and, according to the local press, tackle it they did.

'Messrs. Heywood (Chief Constable), James and Child (Inspectors),' the *Leeds Intelligencer* reported admiringly, 'were indefatigable in their exertions in endeavouring to extinguish the fire and guard the property.'

This was only the latest in a series of rave reviews for the new-fangled force, which had been formed through an amalgamation of the city's 'day police' and 'night watch' in the spring of 1836. In November of that year, the force had distinguished itself in dealing with another major fire, this time in Hunslet.

'The policemen soon restored order and assisted in checking the devouring flames,' the *Leeds Mercury* observed.

The *Mercury* further noted that 'the appearance of novelty in our police has now worn off' and that 'usefulness,

An early fire engine, such as would have attended the scene in Water Lane. (THP)

activity and the prevention of crime have become their prominent characteristics'.

So the 1837 Water Lane fire was just another feather in the force's collective cap, right?

Well...

A few days after the fire – and the glowing report in the *Intelligencer* – the same paper, showing admirable even-handedness, published a letter from four gentlemen of Leeds. In it, the authors pointed out that the facts outlined in the paper's report may have been, in some respects, ever-so-slightly inaccurate. The letter was headlined 'Alleged Misconduct of the Chief Police Officers of Leeds – The late fire in Water Lane'.

Messrs. Matthew Joy, Samuel Smith, John Lord and George Graham claimed that, far from being 'indefatigable in their exertions in endeavouring to extinguish the fire and guard the property', the three officers:'...instead of being so engaged, were drinking and tossing for "grog" at the Malt Shovel Inn, Meadow Lane for upwards of two hours during the time the fire was at its greatest height, and one of them was obliged to go to bed, he being unfit for duty.'

At around four o'clock in the morning, the letter went on, Inspector James finally made it to the site of the fire (Meadow Lane, by the way, is approximately 100 yards from Water Lane). When he got there, he managed to arrest a fireman who had been toiling at the scene for several hours. The fireman was taken to prison, where 'the poor fellow was kept in his wet clothes 'till six o'clock in the morning when he was liberated'.

Showing a talent for understatement, the four signatories to the letter concluded that 'praise has not been bestowed upon the parties most deserving of it'.

Chief Constable Heywood was promptly thrown off the force. But you can't keep a good man down: he was soon launched on a second career as a pawnbroker, and in 1844 was elected a town councillor.

The force would continue to have a shaky relationship with the bottle, in spite of the incentivising assertion in the 1876 'Constable's Guide' that 'strict sobriety is always the first point taken into consideration... when promotions are made'. The brief and inglorious policing career of one James Donelly illuminates the issue eloquently.

The Watch Committee Minutes of 1877 provide the pithy details:

30th November 1877. Watch Committee resolved that they were willing to appoint James Donelly as a police constable on condition that he becomes a total abstainer.

21st December 1877. That James Donelly be appointed police constable.

28th December 1877. That James Donelly be fined 5s. 0d. and severely reprimanded for being drunk on duty.

4th January 1878. That James Donelly be dismissed [from] the force for drunkenness.

As least he made it into the New Year.

AD 1840

TRAGEDY IN ROUNDHAY

WILLIAM NICHOLSON NICHOLSON, Esquire, of Roundhay, north Leeds, was anxious. It was late on a gloomy May night. His wife had woken him – there was a noise at the window, she had said. It sounded like someone was trying to get in.

Nicholson, having risen and dressed hastily, knocked at the door of his groom.

'George,' he called, 'you must get up. There is someone breaking into the house.'

Roundhay, in 1840, was a genteel but isolated suburb of the city, and the Nicholson house was a lonely place, surrounded by the family's extensive grounds. There was no prospect of help: the city's new police force would be of no assistance, not out here, not at this ungodly hour. Whatever was scraping at the window, Nicholson would have to deal with it – with only his groom, George, and his double-barreled shotgun for company.

Nicholson and George stood listening in the quiet house. Suddenly...

'Did you hear that, sir?'

'I did.'

Both had heard a noise as if a man's hand had passed along the bottom of the door.

'I'm sure there is someone about,' said George.

Nicholson, his gun under his arm, gravely handed him a poker.

Nicholson and George crept out into the murky garden. Warily they circled the house. They had good reason to be cautious: it was known that thieves and poachers had recently been abroad in Roundhay, and there had been a rash of attempted housebreakings.

As they approached the front of the house they saw him: a dark figure, hunched in the doorway – prying, Nicholson thought, at the door-hinges.

Nicholson raised his gun, and shouted a warning: 'Holloa! What do you want there?'

No answer. Nicholson drew a bead on the crouched figure, aiming low, and

The mansion in Roundhay Park, home to the Nicholsons and scene of a tragedy in 1840. (THP)

pulled the trigger; the gun kicked and roared, and the dark figure doubled over. *Got him.*

Nicholson and George rushed in to collar the intruder – and then stopped. The man was hurt, but armed; weakly he had raised his gun, and levelled it at George, the groom.

George cried out: 'Oh, keeper, keeper, don't shoot me!'

The figure seemed to hesitate – and William Nicholson Nicholson, Esquire, emptied the second barrel into his guts. The intruder's gun fell to the ground.

As George and Nicholson approached the gloomy doorway, however, it became clear that someone had blundered. They had not, it seemed, been alone in hearing rumours of burglars and thieves abroad in Roundhay – they had not been the only ones prowling the dark gardens in search of trespassers.

From inside the house, Nicholson's wife, listening in terror, heard her husband cry: 'Good gracious, Charles, why didn't you speak?!'

And the weak reply: 'I did not know you, Sir.'

Nicholson had shot forty-nine-year-old Charles Thompson – his own gamekeeper.

Thompson had been horribly wounded in his midriff. In enormous pain, he nevertheless swore on oath that he did not blame Nicholson for shooting him. He also told the groom, George,

that, had George not cried out in terror, both he and Nicholson would have been dead men – only the fact that Thompson recognised George's voice had stayed his trigger-finger.

His story was one of terrible misfortune. He had, he said, been out patrolling the Nicholson property. It was a wet night, and he had taken shelter in the doorway of the Nicholsons' house – a thing he had never done before. He had waited there for two or three hours – until Nicholson had disturbed him.

Others suggested that he had been drinking – that in fact, when he slumped in the dark doorway, he was pretty much dead drunk.

The suffering gamekeeper clung to life through the next day and on into the next night. In the small hours of 20 May, despite the best efforts of local doctors, he succumbed.

What those best efforts involved was made clear at the inquest into the fatal shooting. Examiners inspecting Thompson's body noted that his midriff 'appeared to have perforated in about a dozen places, but it was difficult to say whether they were gunshot wounds or the marks of leeches'.

Nicholson expressed profound regret for his gamekeeper's death. The inquest returned a verdict of 'homicide by misadventure' – meaning that Nicholson was cleared of blame.

AD 1842

THE WORKERS ARE REVOLTING!

YOU COULDN'T CALL Thomas Slingsby Duncombe a man of the people. Yes, he had been born a child of West Yorkshire, son of a Boroughbridge family – but an education that took him to Harrow School and earned him an ensign's commission in the Coldstream Guards had elevated him into the nineteenth-century political elite. Yes, like many working-class families, he often struggled with debts he couldn't pay – but these weren't grocery bills, they were gambling debts, bar tabs, money owed to his tailor (he was known to be the best-dressed man in Westminister).

And yet, when it came to the crunch, Duncombe was prepared to take a stand for the rights of working men and women.

Duncombe was one of the few MPs in the House of Commons of his day who believed that he represented *all* of the people in his constituency, not only those whose wealth, property and status entitled them to vote. As the 1840s dawned, that made Thomas Slingsby Duncombe the right man, in the right place, at precisely the right time.

Britain was on the brink of revolt. The Industrial Revolution had changed the face of the nation. England had a huge population of workers, toiling amid the smoke of great new cities: Manchester, Liverpool, Birmingham, Glasgow – and Leeds. When, in the late 1830s, the economy slumped, conditions for these millions of workers dropped from unpleasant to intolerable.

What could they do about it? Vote in a new government? Well, that was the point: the working men of Britain had no vote; they were disenfranchised, denied the least say in the running of the country whose looms they worked, whose mines they dug, whose steel they forged, and whose cities they built.

So again: what could they do about it? They could, some said, fight.

But many hoped it wouldn't come to that. In May 1838, William Lovett drew up a 'People's Charter', listing six key demands. These demands were designed to tilt the balance of power in Britain away from the outdated 'establishment' and towards the long-suffering workers. They included suffrage for all men, annually elected Parliaments, equal electoral districts and the introduction of pay for MPs (this last measure would mean that a man wouldn't have to be independently wealthy to stand for Parliament).

The working people of Britain rallied behind the 'People's Charter'. The Chartist movement was born.

The Chartists' first assault on Parliament, however, was something of a damp squib. They met in London in July 1839 to present their demands to Parliament in the form of a petition; while Parliament considered the demands, the Chartists muttered darkly about taking 'ulterior measures' if they were not appeased.

Parliament rejected the People's Charter outright. The Chartists, divided over what should be done, did very little.

At least, they did very little until November, when, in a frightening hint

The Chartist riot at Newport. (THP)

of what was to come, the movement's militant leaders staged a violent uprising in the Welsh city of Newport.

The crackdown that followed was inevitable. The rising's leaders were swiftly arrested and deported to the Australian penal colonies; other leading Chartists were also hauled in and thrown into prison. The establishment was making its point forcefully: force, it was clear, would be met with force.

From this point onwards, the Chartists trod rather more carefully. They could afford to, because their campaign for reform was quickly gathering momentum. By the summer of 1842, their petition had some 3.2 million signatures. This, surely, was the voice of the people speaking loud and clear; this, surely, was a demand to which Westminster could not turn a deaf ear.

But the Chartist militants had not gone away – and, if the 'People's Charter' failed a second time, they would know what to do about it. No power on earth would hold them back.

It fell to Thomas Slingsby Duncombe to present the Chartists' demands to Parliament on 4 May 1842. The dapper Duncombe put his case well. His speech commending the petition to the House was said to be 'noble and manly'. It was said to have 'elicited the warm esteem of men of all parties'.

The petition was rejected by 287 votes to 47. At this point, all hell broke loose.

Men working the Midlands coalfields threw down their tools and walked out in protest at Parliment's intransigence. Many said they would not work again until the demands of the Charter were met. The unrest spread quickly, fanned by the militants. Star of the Chartists'

Fire-brand Feargus O'Connor, whose Northern Star *was printed in Leeds. (THP)*

show was the wild Irishman Feargus O'Connor, who roved the country drumming up trouble. He was more than just a loudmouthed rabble-rouser (though he was certainly that); his Chartist newspaper, the *Northern Star*, was one of the country's great newspapers, far outstripping the *Leeds Intelligencer* in terms of circulation and, in the fevered climate of the late 1830s and early 1840s, establishing itself as the mouthpiece of the Radical reformist movement.

It was published by Josiah Hobson from his printing shop on Briggate, Leeds.

From the Midlands' mining towns, the wildcat strike spread to industrial Scotland, and, in the summer of 1842, brought the roaring, rattling, seemingly unstoppable textiles industry of Yorkshire and Lancashire to a halt.

How do you shut down a factory? You simply pull the plug. Removing the plug from a steam boiler was an easy and effective means of crippling a factory's

operations and enforcing strike action. These, then, were the Plug Riots. In August, they came marching into Leeds.

The North, in 1842, was starving. Trade had slumped, unemployment was rife. It was reported that, in Carlisle, a quarter of the city's population was in the grip of famine. The Plug Rioters were not bolshy troublemakers holding the country to ransom for a penny on the pay or an hour off the day. They were desperate. This, they thought, was their final throw of the dice.

It was thought that the North's first Plug Riot broke out among power-loom workers in the Pennine town of Stalybridge, and, like a burst reservoir, spilled out into the valleys to the east and west. In Manchester, some 300 factories were forced to stop work. Town by town, the rebellion spread: Holmfirth, Dewsbury, Halifax, Huddersfield. In Leeds, the mill-owners must have quaked in fear as word spread of the rioters' relentless march eastward. It must have felt like nothing so much as waiting defenceless in the path of an advancing – and hostile – army.

Although 'defenceless' isn't quite the word. Leeds bristled with military authority. Troops were assembled there in force; a legion of special constables – perhaps as many as 1,500 – had been sworn in. When, on the morning of 17 August, word arrived that a detachment of Plug Rioters had left Bradford and were heading along the road to Leeds, the city, it seemed, was more than ready for them.

The anticipated ruckus was meat-and-drink to Feargus O'Connor's *Northern Star*. Every week, the packed columns of the paper were alive with feverish rhetoric – 'They have raised a devil they will find it difficult to lay!!' and 'THEY MUST AND SHALL STAND ERECT AS FREE MEN'– and upbeat bulletins detailing strikes, set-tos, raucous Chartist meetings and anti-establishment riots. The news came from Bingley and Burslem, Hanley and Heckmondwike, Dewsbury and Dunfermline, Stafford and Stockport, Wigan and Wakefield – everywhere, in fact, where men earned their livings with their hands, their backs and the sweat of their brow.

The first bulletin from the *Star*'s Leeds correspondent was dramatic: 'On Saturday [August 13] this town was thrown into a state of great excitement,' he wrote, 'on learning that the operatives' strike had extended from Lancashire into Yorkshire and was making rapid progress in all the Western districts of the county.'

Leeds was the hub of the authorities' military response to the march of the Chartists. From here, one troop of the 17th Lancers was despatched to Halifax, and a second to Huddersfield; troops of Yeomanry Cavalry marched to York and Gildersome; a company of the 87th Foot was sent to quell the unrest in Bradford.

On the Monday, Leeds' anxious mill owners were summoned to a council of war. Many enrolled as special constables. A Royal Proclamation calling for peace was widely circulated in a bid to steady the nerves of the townspeople. Pubs were ordered to close at 8 p.m. Thirty thousand truncheons were ordered for the new special constables. And all the while, a steady drip-drip-drip of scare stories came from the west: Hussars killed or captured by the Chartists in Elland,

bloody clashes between Chartists and the army in Huddersfield and Halifax...

On Tuesday, a number of Leeds Chartists gathered at Hunslet Moor, a little way south of the city. This was a meeting, not a riot – the Chartists discussed their plans and reiterated their support for the People's Charter. Then the meeting was disbanded. These were only local campaigners, not the fearsome mob that was descending from the Pennines – that was, indeed, now advancing on the suburbs of west Leeds.

Bramley, Pudsey, Stanningley, Fulneck and Calverley lay in the marchers' path. Each mill that they passed was summarily shut down. As the workers from each mill were turned out, the Chartists' numbers swelled: by the time the mob reached Stanningley, they numbered perhaps 6,000.

Their first priority was not to fight. It was to eat. 'Hunger seemed to be the great mover of the painful drama,' the *Northern Star* reported. 'The Butchers' shops were visited, and the meat that was given to them was devoured in a raw state.'

At Pudsey, the size of the mob was estimated at 8,000 to 10,000. Unsurprisingly, most of the mill owners in the district shut down without a fight. One, however, held out. He was the owner of Banks' Mill in Far Pudsey. He stubbornly refused the Chartists' demands – at which the Chartists, as the *Star* put it, 'began the work of destruction'.

The authorities – hell-bent on maintaining the security of central Leeds – responded weakly. A handful of soldiers from the 17th Hussars were sent out to tackle the vast mob. The Riot Act was read; the Chartists were given a few moments to disperse.

They did not disperse. They took a look at the soldiers (all fourteen of them), made some quick calculations, and charged. The Hussars were routed – and sent on their way by a hail of stones thrown by the Chartists.

The *Star* was at pains to point out that, if the owner of Banks' Mill had only done as he was told, there needn't have been any trouble at all. All the Chartists wanted was to stop the mills and get outside a square meal.

On this latter point, the paper was quick to praise the touching generosity of the locals.

Food, wrote the *Star*'s man on the spot, 'was given readily and generously by every party called upon – rich as well as poor'. 'Several persons who had been thus visited declared they did not begrudge their contributions,' he added. 'Some who had previously declared they would not give a morsel of bread or a farthing of money were touched by the congregated mass of misery which presented itself, and could not withhold assistance from their apparently famishing fellow-creatures.'

With the mighty mills of west Leeds silenced and their bellies full, the Chartists' work was seemingly done. They turned, and began the walk back to Bradford.

But this was far from the last act of the drama.

In the early evening, in industrial Holbeck, only a short step across the river from the heart of the city, another mob was mustering – another Plug Riot was brewing. From Holbeck Moor Road they marched north, turning out workers and stopping mills as they went. They soon reached one of the grandest mills in the city: Marshall's.

This six-storey flax-spinning plant, built in the early 1790s by the Briggate-born industrial magnate John Marshall, loomed over Holbeck. At its peak, 2,000 people were employed to work its 7,000 steam-powered spindles.

By the standards of the day, Marshall was a benevolent employer. He forbade corporal punishment of his workers – although there may have been lapses: in 1832 it was alleged that 'in Mr Marshall's mill, a boy of 9 years of age was stripped to the skin, bound to an iron pillar, and mercilessly beaten with straps, until he fainted'. He made attempts to regulate the temperature of the mill, and sent some of his workers' children to a school he established in the district. He was far from the stereotype of the grasping, heartless mill-owner whose only concerns were raking in cash and grinding the faces of the poor.

The mill's yard-door, which led to the boilers, was barricaded and manned by John Marshall and an army of his workmen. But it was not enough to hold back the mob: they stormed the gate, and flooded into the mill-yard.

But they could not strike at the mill's heart – they could not find the boiler-plugs. Deflated, the Chartists withdrew – only to stumble into the hands of the authorities.

A party of Lancers met the mob on Water Lane. At the head of the cavalry rode Prince George, grandson to George III. They took on the Chartists at full speed, quickly isolating their leaders; for the second time in Leeds that day, the Riot Act was read.

Inside Marshall's Mill at around the time of the Chartist unrest. (By kind permission of the Leeds Library and Information Service)

Uniforms were everywhere: Fusiliers, Hussars, Lancers, police. Even the city's magistrates were out on patrol. The mob was stilled, stymied.

But not for long. No sooner had Prince George withdrawn his troops than the Chartists were up to their old plug-pulling tricks again. A lightning raid on Benyon's Water Lane flax mill brought the mill grinding to a halt and the workers out on strike, and then on marched the mob.

At the end of Dewsbury Road they ran up against a troop of police and special constables. These were no Lancers; Chief Constable Read was no Prince George. Stones filled the air. Fists flew. Battle was joined.

But George's Lancers were soon along to restore order and round up the troublemakers: altogether, the thirty-eight Chartists were arrested. It was to be the last hurrah of the Leeds Chartists that summer.

AD 1844

SOLDIERS DECLARE WAR

– on the Police!

IT'S HARD TO BELIEVE, but members of this country's armed forces – the army, in particular – haven't always been quite the most popular public figures in the towns and cities of England. Rudyard Kipling summed up the prevailing sentiment in his 1892 poem *Tommy*:

> I went into a public 'ouse to get a pint o' beer.
> The publican 'e up and sez, 'We serve no redcoats 'ere.'
> ...
> It's Tommy this, an' Tommy that, an' Tommy, go away;
> But it's 'Thank you, Mister Atkins', when the band begins to play.

One public 'ouse where the Tommies of the British Army were wont to enjoy numerous pints o' beer was Ben Brooksbank's Green Man on York Street, central Leeds. It was a regular haunt of the gentlemen of the 70th Infantry, stationed at Woodhouse Lane. They had a decent reputation in the city, or at least as decent as could be expected: fewer of them had been hauled up before the magistrates than had been the case with

previous corps stationed in Leeds. But it was at the Green Man that they would cement their lasting unpopularity – not, it has to be said, without considerable provocation.

The problems began on the evening of 8 January 1844. It isn't clear what had put the squaddies of the 70th in such a foul temper that night. The *Leeds Intelligencer* reported that tensions were high because the police had broken up a weekly 'gathering and harangue' of temperance campaigners and social activists at Vicar's Croft Market that afternoon. Others suggested that the fuse had been lit by a piece of incendiary graffiti: on a wooden table in the Green Man, someone had scratched the words, 'No swaddy Irishmen or soldiers wanted here'.

Whatever the cause, Edward Thompson, a stranger in town, chose the wrong night to stroll into the Green Man, call for a drink, and lay his money on the counter.

There were two men of the 70th, John Karin and John Brian, loitering at the bar. One or the other pocketed Thompson's money. Thompson – understandably if not wisely – protested.

Boar Lane, where Leeds' Trevelyan Temperance Hotel can be seen (named after Sir Walter Trevelyan, president of the UK Temperance Alliance). The breaking up of a Temperance meeting was one of the factors that sparked the riot. (THP)

The soldiers took offence: they promptly set about the unfortunate stranger.

The melee spilled out of the pub into the street. One of the soldiers, showing great resourcefulness, dashed into a nearby brothel and seized a poker from among the fire-irons. Returning to the fray, he struck Thompson a fierce blow on the head. Blood splashed the cobbles. Thompson fell senseless.

Nor were Karin and Brian in any mood to repent their hot-headedness. When two police constables, PCs Best and Haight, arrived, the soldiers insisted that they had 'served him right' – and that, moreover, they'd give him some more, given half a chance.

They were not to be given half a chance. Best and Haight duly took the brawling squaddies into custody.

It was while the pair were being escorted across town that the real trouble began.

As the four men crossed Kirkgate, a mob of soldiers emerged from the shadows of Wharf Street. At their head was one Sherburd, a soldier of the 70th. Confronting the officers, he meaningfully undid his belt, motioning for his fellows to do the same. The belt, made from heavy leather and fastened with a stout brass buckle, was the squaddies' weapon of choice in a street fight.

As the mob – all, with the exception of Sherburd, roaring drunk – fell upon the helpless constables, Brian and Karin broke loose. The officers' whistles shrieked: Kirkgate, at that time, was busy with coppers, and reinforcements soon arrived.

The fighting became, as they say, general.

Flying belt-buckles crashed against the policemen's truncheons. Huge crowds gathered to watch the battle – 'the commotion was very great,' said the *Intelligencer*, surely not overstating the case.

When the dust settled, Brian and Karin had been recaptured – and three other soldiers of the 70th had been collared, too.

The arraignments that followed the next morning shed a little light on the relations that existed between soldiers and townspeople.

Markland, the magistrate, remarked with regret that there existed 'a practice... of using insulting language against soldiers', and voiced hopes that such practice would soon be stamped out.

The belligerent soldier Sherburd put it more colourfully. Asked if he could produce any witnesses to corroborate his version of the previous night's events, he said that the only people present had been civilians – and there was not one among them who wouldn't rather plunge a knife into a soldier than assist him.

The remark drew cheers from Sherburd's supporters in the public gallery. *No one likes us, we don't care* about sums it up. The 70th Infantry were not men of Leeds. They had no close ties with the city. And if the local coppers wanted trouble, the 70th were ready to make sure they got it. By Monday evening, the soldiers who weren't already banged up had, in the *Intelligencer's* limpid prose, 'concocted an effective plan for gratifying their revengeful propensity'.

In other words, it was open season on the city's police force.

The soldiers fortified themselves for the evening's planned activities by congregating in two mobs at the Green Man and another pub, the Green Parrot on Harper Street (just off Kirkgate). Then they headed out into the town.

Police Constable Sam Smith had the misfortune to be the first policemen the marauding soldiers came across. They began by knocking off his hat. They followed up by beating him half-senseless. 'Damn him, kill him!' Smith heard someone shout.

Wielding belts, bludgeons and sticks, some forty or fifty soldiers advanced on Briggate, the main shopping thoroughfare. As they marched, they waved their brutal-looking 2ft sticks in the air. Shopkeepers hurriedly boarded up their shops at the sound of the mob's approach. Others, however, egged on the mob: at least one man was seen to raise his hat and cry, 'Go on, lads!' The *Intelligencer* described the city centre as being in 'much the same crowded and excited state as... during the plug-drawing riots of 1842'.

The violence was short and sharp. Soldiers hunted down police officers across the city centre. Yells of 'bloody Peelers!' – and no doubt worse – rang out; one soldier reportedly yelled, 'We'll murder them all!'

The policemen's bleak situation was made worse when members of the public pitched in on the soldiers' side (the police, at the time, were perhaps the only men less popular in Leeds than the soldiers).

Then reinforcements arrived: extra policemen scattered the mobs, and a military piquet from the Woodhouse

Lane barracks rounded them up. Six officers were left 'desperately wounded'. Fourteen soldiers and nine civilians would answer for their bloody night's work in court.

Even with the brawlers of the 70th confined to barracks, anti-police sentiment continued to fester. The Tuesday night saw gangs of factory lads harassing officers on patrol, flinging abuse, sticks and bottles. The officers responded by wearing their scabbarded cutlasses in plain sight. The rabble soon got the message, and dispersed: peace, at last, returned to the town centre.

At the trial, the city's mayor described the violence as 'an outrage unexampled in the history of the borough, both in point of audacity and brutality'. A witness who had lived on Kirkgate for twenty-six years said that he had never seen that part of the town in 'so alarming a state'.

Four soldiers were convicted by the court. Three – McGlenaghan, Coghlan and Mooran – received eight months apiece; the fourth, William O'Brien, was targeted by the prosecution as a ringleader, and was given a year.

One civilian – waiter Manasseh Flatow – was fined £4 for his part in the fighting; three others got away lightly, with the court recommending mercy.

The local press was predictably fierce in its condemnation of the rioting.

'It is impossible to conceive a more alarming state of society than that which was witnessed in this town during the existence of the riot on Monday night,' the *Leeds Mercury* declared. 'We look in vain for any adequate cause for this act of military licence.'

But in truth the riots were simply the result of grievances that had simmered for months finally coming to a boil. The competing prejudices form a complicated knot, almost impossible to unpick. The police were interfering bullies. The soldiers were boozy troublemakers. Added to this was a spike of racial tension: it was no accident that the Green Man graffiti lumped together 'Irishmen and soldiers', for the men of the 70th were widely thought of as Irish (in fact, most of them came from the South of England – but it was true that most of those arrested were at least of Irish heritage). The Sunday afternoon police intervention at Vicar's Croft Market had, the *Intelligencer* said, stirred up anti-police feeling among 'the Irish, teetotallers and Chartists'. The city was a powder keg. The innocuous James Thompson, the Green Man's most unfortunate customer, was the only spark it had needed to go *bang*.

AD 1864

SARGISSON AND MYERS DANCE THE LAST WALTZ

RELATIVELY FEW PUBLIC executions took place in Leeds. If you wanted to watch a hanging – as many did – York was really the place to be. But when they *did* happen in Leeds, the people turned out in force. The murderer Holroyd, as we have seen, drew a crowd of some 30,000 to Holbeck Moor in 1682, but even he was outdone when, in September 1864, Armley Gaol staged its first – and last – public execution.

The grim and forbidding gaol had been built in 1847 and was the main repository for West Yorkshire's robbers, killers and other wrong 'uns. Its soot-blackened turrets loomed ominously over west Leeds.

On 10 September, the two men who were to be hanged in the gaol's shadow were dragged out to the gallows. Their names were James Sargisson and Joseph Myers. Gathered there to watch them was a crowd of perhaps 100,000 souls.

Armley Gaol. (By kind permission of the Leeds Library and Information Service)

THE BALLAD OF JOSEPH AND JAMES

Such was the festive atmosphere among the multitude gathered to watch Myers and Sargisson hang that a printed ballad-sheet was circulated, bearing the words to a specially-written song.

It began with Myers' imagined lament:

Within a dark and dreary dungeon,
I for mercy now do cry,
For killing of my own dear Nancy
At Armley Jail I am doomed to die...

There were six verses of this sort of thing. A chorus warned against allowing temptation to lead men on to the 'cursed drink' that had supposedly been Myers' downfall.

Halfway through, the ballad turned its attention to Sargisson:

James Sargisson but aged twenty,
Is with Joseph Myers doomed to die,
At Laughton he did slay John Cooper,
And he must reach the gallows high.

It isn't known whether the song was ever sung.

It was not, of course, the first or last execution to be held at Armley – only the first and last *public* one. Many had already been despatched to their maker in the bleak privacy of the gaol's inner cells; many more would be in the years to follow.

Among them was the Sheffield murderer Joseph Laycock, who on the gallows in 1884 asked the hangman: 'You will not hurt me?' – to which the hangman reportedly replied, 'Nay, tha'll nivver feel it, for tha'll be out of existence i' two minutes.' Another was John Johnson, who in 1877 was hanged for killing a friend in a drunken fit of jealousy. In fact, Johnson was hanged twice: on the first attempt, the rope broke; even on the second, the kill was not clean, and Johnson was seen to struggle on the rope for some four

agonising minutes. His incompetent hangman, Thomas Askern, was never invited back to Armley.

A botched execution such as Johnson's was only one of many potential diverting happenings that could enliven a public hanging. A cold-blooded murderer might repent on the gallows – even better, he might cry. Or there might be some stirring last words.

And of course a *double* hanging, such as the Armley crowd had gathered to watch, promised twice the entertainment.

James Sargisson had been convicted of murdering a man named John Cooper during a robbery in Rotherham, South Yorkshire, in April. Sargisson – who confessed to his involvement after the government offered a £100 reward – blamed the killing on an accomplice,

The horrible murder of his wife with a pair of scissors sent a man to the Leeds gallows. (THP)

one Denton. He protested that Denton had coerced him into robbing Cooper, that Denton had killed the man, and that Denton had then ordered him, Sargisson, to conceal the dead man's stolen watch and keys in his pig-sty.

It was to no avail. Denton was acquitted. Sargisson was sentenced to hang.

The man who was to join him on the Armley gallows, meanwhile, was guilty of a yet grislier crime. In June, a policeman, called to a house in Sheffield, found Elizabeth Myers bleeding to death, and her husband, Joseph, sat nearby. Myers had cut his own throat, and was bleeding horribly, but still managed to say to the constable: 'I have done it, and I hope the bitch will die. I stabbed her with the scissors blade.'

As he was taken away, he again voiced his wish that his wife would die – adding that 'all I feel sorry for is the children'.

Repeatedly he had tried to re-open the wound he had made in his own throat – to 'cheat the hangman' by taking his own life. But the surgeons of the infirmary put a stop to that, sewing him up and coating the wound with plaster. Myers would die not when he chose but when the law demanded. Justice would be done.

The crowd had begun to gather at Armley on the Friday evening, with the hangings scheduled for the next day. By Saturday, every available space was filled with eager spectators: they jostled on the rooftops of nearby mills and houses, and shinned up walls and lampposts. Crowds even formed at far-off Burley Road and Woodhouse Moor, in little hope of seeing anything much but wanting, in any case, to partake of the carnival atmosphere.

Mostly they were mill-hands, factory workers, artisans. The Leeds *Mercury* reported that there were many 'drawn from a lower and more degraded stratum of society' than that, but also that a number of 'the respectable class' were present to watch the two men die.

The paper also noted that there were many women among the spectators, a number of whom were carrying babies. Their anxiety to get 'a good view', the paper observed, 'exceeded that of the men'.

Scripture readers, balanced on stools below the gallows, read solemn lessons from the Bible as the hour of the execution drew near. Many of the spectators listened respectfully. Others did not. There were jokes, heckles, banter. Some men were even seen to be playing games – 'thimblerig' and 'fly the garter' – to pass the time.

Canon Edward Jackson, a clergyman who had tended to Myers and Sargisson as they prepared for the gallows, later recalled the scene.

'What a sad, and I may say horrible, picture of humanity was then exhibited,' he lamented. 'I allude not to the wretched culprits so much, as to the fact of the vast crowd gathered together to gaze on their dying agonies, and the utterly revolting deportment showed by the larger portion of those comprising it.'

Then the prisoners appeared. Both looked exhausted. Sargisson, in fact, had had to be given stimulants to make it this far. Of the two, Myers seemed the more resigned to his dismal fate.

As the dull gaol bell began to toll, the hangman tied the murderers' hands behind their backs. Mr Tuckwell, the chaplain, intoned the funeral service. On the previous Sunday, Tuckwell had delivered a 'condemned sermon' to some 380 Armley prisoners – Myers and Sargisson among them.

It had not been heartening stuff.

'My brethren,' Tuckwell had said, 'this is the last Lord's day which two of you can expect to spend on earth. When another Sabbath morn shall dawn, you will be numbered with the dead.'

Now, as he spoke on the gallows, the two condemned men were rapt. Several times they were heard to cry out, 'Lord save me!' and 'Lord save my soul!'

Tuckwell pronounced absolution. Forward stepped the hangman, and draped white hoods over the two men's heads.

Sargisson turned to Myers.

'Art th' 'appy, lad?' he asked.

'Yes, I am,' was Myers' reply – the last words he would ever speak.

The crowd waited in silence. The traps opened. *Thud.* The two men fell – vanished from the sight of the crowd.

Beneath the platform, Joseph Myers lay dead at the end of his rope. The wound in his throat had been ripped open; blood drenched his clothes and pooled on the floor beneath. Sargisson, however, was not dead; he struggled, gasping, in his noose – but not for long.

As was customary, the two dead men hung from their ropes for an hour, during which the screens were drawn back to demonstrate to the crowd that justice – a bleak, ugly, violent justice – had been done. Then they were cut down.

People would continue to be executed at Armley for many years to come – the last was Zsiga Pankotia, almost a century later, in 1961. But there would never again be such a crowd assembled to see it done: in 1868, public executions were outlawed by an Act of Parliament.

The black turrets of Armley would not see the like of this again.

AD 1865

DISORDER, DEATH AND DRIPPING

IN THE SNOWY WINTER of 1865, Park Square, near the city centre, was the site of what is perhaps the most stereotypically northern outbreak of civil unrest ever recorded in Yorkshire. The Leeds Dripping Riots are rivalled only by the Great Lard Butty Massacre of 1745 in their ability to conjure an image of the Northerner as a scurvy-ridden, whey-faced nutritional basket-case.

And the Dripping Riots, unlike the Lard Butty Massacre, actually happened.

A note for gastronomes and Southerners may be necessary at this point. Dripping is the flavoursome fat that drips from a joint of meat during roasting. It can still be bought in many butchers' shops, is often spread on bread as a tasty snack, and is known to connoisseurs as 'mucky fat'.

Eliza Stafford obviously had a taste for it. In January 1865, she was brought before the city magistrates, charged with the theft of 2lb – about 900g – of the stuff. The dripping had been pilfered from the kitchen of Mr Henry Chorley, a prominent surgeon and magistrate, who employed Eliza as a kitchen maid. Eliza's defence – that she had stolen the fat with 'charitable intent' – didn't wash; she was sentenced to a month in Armley Prison.

Cue uproar.

Graffiti began to appear on walls and buildings throughout the city: 'Chorley's dripping' was a typical daubing. The *Leeds Intelligencer* reported that 'Mr Chorley... has been subjected to every possible annoyance'. He was sent abusive letters and was assailed with dripping-themed verbal abuse whenever he took to the streets. 'How's thy fat, lad?' people would demand; others would simply cry 'Dripping! Dripping!'

Chorley took this abuse in good part; in fact, his robustness was such that it has been suggested that he partially incited the disturbances that followed.

Word of Eliza Stafford's ordeal spread far beyond the city, thanks in part to the *Leeds Express* championing the cook's cause. The *Times* of London picked up the story; in Liverpool, one paper ran the headline 'How They Treat Their Cooks in Leeds'. The affair even merited a column in New Zealand's *Otago Daily Times*.

The mounting drama came to a head on 22 February, the morning of Eliza's release. A great crowd – possibly as many as 10,000 – gathered in the cold, snowy

Park Square today. (Catherine Bale)

streets in the shadow of the prison's forbidding turrets. They were there to welcome their ill-treated heroine: Eliza was to be paraded in triumph through the city streets.

Except that Eliza, mortified by the fuss she had caused, had already been released. She had been sneaked out of a side-door at daybreak and was already on her way to Scarborough – where, according to some reports, she planned to spend a quiet life as landlady of a pub called 'The Dripping Pan'.

Chief Constable Bell of the city police had the unenviable duty of announcing to the mob that their long, cold wait had been in vain. He was promptly and cheerfully buried in a flurry of snowballs. Further hilarity followed when a tall man in women's clothing appeared before the mob, claiming to be their beloved Eliza. Everyone remained in good humour; they would have their fun regardless.

Around 1,000 people regrouped later in the day outside Mr Chorley's fashionable residence in Park Square. It seems to have been a rather jovial gathering. The *Intelligencer* reported sniffily that song-sheets of disrespectful ballads 'sold amazingly well'.

Sing-songs notwithstanding, though, there was a whiff of trouble in the air. The crowd swelled as the protestors were joined by local workers on their lunch-breaks. City officials, the *Intelligencer* reported, had a 'strong apprehension that... the question of a cook's right to the perquisite of a dripping-pan would lead to further tumult'. At 2 p.m., the Town Hall issued a proclamation ordering the mob to 'disperse and depart'.

It didn't work. So the city sent in the police. Or, as the *Intelligencer* approvingly put it, 'repressive measures, such as a placid exercise of magisterial authority naturally shrinks from, [were] promptly put in force'.

Scarborough, where Eliza Stafford retired after the dripping debacle. (Courtesy of the Library of Congress, LC-DIG-ppmsc-09065)

THE SINGING RIOTERS

The lyrics of the satirical songs bellowed by the Park Square mob weren't exactly subtle. They did, however, get the protestors' point across. And belting them out at window-shaking volume was probably a good way of keeping warm.

> Oh, if I was the doctor [one satirical song went], I would let them see,
> I'd take an example from Victor Townley.
> If ever I dealt out such justice again,
> I'd jump from my seat and fracture my brain.

Victor Townley was a notorious murderer of the day who, ten days before, had jumped from a high staircase in Pentonville prison, landed on his head, and died.

Another raucous anti-Chorley song was written in Leeds dialect:

> Nah t'month e Armley jail is past,
> An she cums aght agean at last,
> While throo each road an' lane an' street,
> The public this poor servant meet,
> An' show their luv ov truth an' right
> Ageean this wod-be man of might!

It concluded with the rousing if slightly mystifying chorus: 'Drippin', drippin', drippin'! Noa perquisite nor tippin'!'.

Sticks and stones were now being thrown by the restive mob. The unfortunate Chief Constable Bell, advancing on the protestors, slipped in the snow, and broke his arm (no doubt to the mob's amusement). Then events took a darker turn: a police charge panicked the mob, and a local potter, George Hodgson, fell amid the stampede and was horribly trampled. He died soon afterwards.

By now, dusk was falling. The crowd had shifted its attentions to the Town Hall and was serenading the city fathers within with a chorus of hooting ('and other dismal noises,' the *Intelligencer* noted). The police continued to get it in the neck: proceeding up Calverley Street, truncheons in hand, they were pelted with stones and many were painfully bloodied.

As reported in the *Intelligencer* afterwards, one ruffian, collared by a Detective Northcliffe, went so far as to call the officer 'a silly ___'.

Impatient, Bell sent for back-up: police officers from Bradford and soldiers from the garrison at York. These men of the 8th Hussars were battle-hardened veterans. Perhaps mercifully for the protestors, they were never deployed. The Dripping Riots petered out.

In the aftermath, five teenagers were charged with 'riotous conduct'. One, Samuel Baker, a local baker 'of bad character', was sentenced to a week in jail. Magistrates spoke indulgently of 'very silly excitement, which led into disturbance unintended'.

More severe were the judgments of the conservative press. In a broader political sense, the timing of the riot could hardly have been more unfortunate. In Westminster, the heated debate over the franchise – whether or not to extend the vote to the 'lower classes' – was at fever pitch.

The conservative *Intelligencer* saw in the hooting, snowballing, stone-throwing Dripping Rioters an excellent opportunity to put the boot into the universal suffrage movement.

In particular, they trained their guns on Leeds MP Edward Baines. Baines' father, also Edward, had been the proprietor of the rival *Leeds Mercury*. The younger Edward had edited the newspaper, maintaining a strong liberal stance on social issues, before following his father and elder brother into Parliament.

He was no Radical. Baines did not demand that *all* men be given the vote – still less that the franchise be extended to (horror of horrors!) women. All he proposed was that the property requirement be lowered from £10 to £6.

But even this went too far for the *Intelligencer*. The paper and its readers did not share Baines' faith in the basic respectability of the artisan class.

Two letters published in the paper in the days following the riot reflect the repugnance felt by the city's privileged middle classes towards the members of the Dripping Riot mob: 'On the very evening that their champion [Mr Baines] is pleading their cause in the House of Commons... the "intelligent working classes" are preparing for the riot of

Edward Baines. (THP)

the morrow,' wrote 'A Liberal Burgess'. 'It surely becomes every householder who has a wife and family... to protect to reflect on the consequences of placing the franchise in the hands of men who are so easily led away by their passions and prejudices in the manner we have just seen.'

A second correspondent, 'Justitia', gleefully pointed out that the mob had been composed not of the poverty-racked 'underclass' but 'of that very class whom our friend Baines is so anxious to admit to the franchise'.

While not exactly a PR masterstroke, the Dripping Riots did not do any lasting harm – except to poor George Hodgson and his family. Only two years later, Benjamin Disraeli made his 'great leap in the dark': the 1867 Reform Bill, a measure too radical even for Baines, gave the vote to every male householder in England.

AD 1884

THE PHANTOM IN
THE LIBRARY

LEEDS, LIKE EVERY CITY, has its share of ghost stories. But not many ghost stories are as creepily detailed as that recounted by the young Leeds librarian John MacAlister in 1884. And few encounters with the walking dead take place in a location as evocative as the 250-year-old Leeds Library.

The library was founded in 1768; the legendary chemist Joseph Priestley was one of its first subscribers. The library moved from place to place for a number of years, before, in 1808, finally settling in first-floor premises on Commercial Street, in the centre of the city.

It still stands there today. It remains an extraordinary place, musty and quiet, a repository of ancient volumes, a warren of shadowy corners, winding staircases, endless cellars and lonely galleries.

Into this strange world of learning and lore came John MacAlister. In May 1880, aged just twenty-four, MacAlister was appointed the library's head librarian. For four years he worked in the quiet chambers without incident: arranging the ancient collections, advising scholars, perhaps taking time to repair loose pages or flaking book-bindings.

For some reason, his work kept him late at the library one evening in March 1884. So late, in fact, that he suddenly realised that was in danger of missing his last train home to Harrogate. Grabbing his things and snatching up a lamp, he dashed from his office.

As he hastened through the dark library, the lamp he was carrying suddenly, and startlingly, illuminated a man's face at the end of a gloomy passageway.

A burglar, John supposed. Heart pounding, he ran back to his office – and returned with a loaded revolver.

Joseph Priestley, the famous 'Chemical Philosopher', who was one of the haunted library's first subscribers; he was also the man who discovered oxygen. (Courtesy of the Library of Congress, LC-USZ62-44066)

In the dusty silence of the library, he shouted a warning – more in the faint hope that a policeman passing by in the street outside might hear him and come to his aid than in any expectation of rousting the intruder. No answer. He shouted again – his quavering voice echoed among the high, dark shelves.

No answer.

Then, from behind a bookcase, the face reappeared. It was no burglar.

The face was pallid and hairless, with deep, heavily shadowed eye-sockets. Hesitantly, gripping the butt of his revolver, MacAlister advanced toward it. Now he saw not only a face but a body – an old man's body, tall, with high shoulders – and seeming, as MacAlister watched in amazement, to rotate out of the end of the bookcase. The figure turned its back on MacAlister. Moving with a strange, shuffling gait, it walked quickly away from the bookcase, and went into the library's small lavatory.

MacAlister followed the figure – and found that it had vanished. There was no trace of anyone in the tiny room.

'I confess I began to experience for the first time what novelists describe as an "eerie" feeling,' the librarian later remembered.

It was a local priest, Charles Hargrove, who, on hearing John MacAlister's disturbing tale, identified the strange, hairless figure as one Vincent Sternberg, John's predecessor as librarian. Sternberg matched MacAlister's description of the library ghost: he had lost all his hair in a gunpowder blast, and since the accident had walked with a shuffling gait. Sternberg had died several months previously.

This was not the end of the haunting of the Leeds Library. Sternberg's ghost continued, it seems, to linger among the old books.

Librarians working at the library after dark reported extinguished lamps being mysteriously re-lit in Sternberg's old office. MacAlister himself noticed an even stranger phenomenon: odd, resonant vibrations issuing from a long library table. These were attributed to 'Sternberg's gong': the old librarian had been accustomed to keep a gong on that table, which he would strike when he needed a colleague's assistance.

In 1885 things began to get out of hand. A group of young librarians, in adventurous mood, convened a seánce, determined to make definite contact with the restless spirit of Vincent Sternberg.

Afterwards, they reported that Sternberg, communicating through knocking sounds, had brushed aside the veil and emerged from the Other Side to make a terrible confession: sometimes, when head librarian, he had given away library books to friends.

At a later seánce, the irritable ghost provoked a former head librarian into accusing him of fiddling the library's accounts.

Boyish pranks, no doubt. Nevertheless, it seems that hairless, shuffling, gong-striking Vincent Sternberg had managed to get well and truly under his successor's skin. One afternoon, as 'Sternberg's gong' again rang out eerily in the library reading room, library employee Albert Edmunds urged John MacAlister to commune with the spirit in private, and learn its secrets once and for all.

'I have suffered enough from that man's misdeeds,' MacAlister snapped in reply, 'and if he's in Hell, he deserves to be.

THE RESTLESS DEAD OF LEEDS

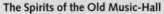

Charlie Peace

Sheffield-born Charlie Peace was thick-featured, heavy-jawed and short in stature; he had three missing fingers, and walked with a limp – a legacy from a steel-mill apprenticeship. He was skilled at two things: playing the violin, and burglary. He roved Victorian England, womanising, playing his fiddle in pubs and robbing the homes of the gentry. He killed at least twice. In 1878, he was finally nabbed – betrayed by his mistress for a £100 reward. In the winter of 1879, at Armley Prison, Charlie Peace was hanged by the neck until he was dead. Dead, but perhaps not gone: it's said that today the unquiet ghost of the murderer lingers in the dank prison cells that can still be explored beneath Leeds Town Hall.

Charles Peace attempting to murder Constable Robinson. (THP)

The Spirits of the Old Music-Hall

The City Varieties wasn't the first theatre in Leeds – the city has been home to playhouses of one sort or another since the 1720s – but for a long time it was the best known. It was built in 1865 as an extension to the music room of the White Swan inn; the pub might be gone, but the Varieties is still there. It's said to be home to both a courtly, debonair ghost in a bowler hat, and to the spirit of a lady actress. One eerie tale tells of a theatre *impresario* who fell asleep, drunk, in the Varieties' bar, and was accidentally locked in overnight. In the small hours, he woke in confusion from his uneasy sleep – to find the lady standing over him.

The 'Blue Lady'

Every fine old family should have a dark tragedy in its past, and every stately home should have a ghost. The Ingrams can tell of poor Mary Ingram, daughter of Sir Arthur Ingram; Mary was only a girl when, in 1652, she was subjected to a terrifying attack on the highway, suffered a breakdown, and died. And Temple Newsam, the magnificent estate in east Leeds that was the Ingrams' family home, now boasts of the 'Blue Lady' – the ghost of Mary Ingram, who is said to stalk the house's halls and galleries.

The Abbey Inn

In Newlay, near Horsforth, stands an ancient hostelry with a claim to be the most ghost-ridden pub in the city. The Abbey Inn has been licensed since 1834 – but, for much of its history, it was more than just a pub. Throughout the nineteenth and early twentieth centuries, the Abbey doubled as the village mortuary...

AD 1910

PANIC IN THE PARK

RUGBY WAS A tough game in Victorian England. These were the days when 'indiscriminate hacking' – i.e. whaling on an opponent's shins with boots and studs – was an essential part of the game; when one correspondent could report that 'arms, legs, collar-bones, knees, ankles were constantly broken, dislocated or fractured' – and in a schoolboy match.

Rule changes in the 1870s might have smoothed off some of the game's most fearsomely jagged edges, but the fact remained that the Victorian rugby field was no place for milksops.

This was particularly true in the North. Rugby, a game that in the South was dominated by university and school teams, was in Lancashire and especially Yorkshire a more blue-collar pursuit. The founding clubs of the Yorkshire Rugby Union in 1888 sprang in the main from the industrial suburbs: Wortley, Hunslet, Holbeck, Bramley.

This was the world in which James Arthur Miller made his name. In the 1870s he played for Leeds St John's – the precursor of today's Leeds Rhinos – as a forward, deep in the 'tight scrimmage' and on the front line of the on-going

debate over the safety of hacking. In retirement, he earned greater fame with his skilful handling of the sport's prickly politics: Miller fought for the right of working players to claim compensation for the time they spent away from the mill or foundry (though in the end he declined to side with the breakaway Rugby Football League when the matter came to a head in 1895).

But Miller was to face a new and terrible challenge in the summer of 1910.

A rather grey spring had given way to a lacklustre summer in Leeds. In May, the death of the king – the boozy, portly, well-liked Edward VII – had brought his son George V to the throne. The local atmosphere was unsettled: workers in the region's keystone wool industry had gone on strike, agitating for higher pay.

In the pleasant north Leeds suburb of Roundhay, though, nothing but a day of jolly entertainment seemed to be on the cards. The famous Roundhay Park, a popular destination for day-trippers and charabancs since its opening as a public park in 1872, was to host a grand gala in aid of the Leeds Lifeboat Society. The gala was to conclude with a spectacular firework display.

THE RUGBY RUMPUS.

Caricatures of James Miller, wounded during the accident, and the Revd Frank Marshall, an arch-opponent of 'broken-time payments'. That caption reads: Marshall: 'Oh, fie, go away naughty boy, I don't play with boys who can't afford to take a holiday for football any day they like!' Miller: 'Yes, that's just you to a T; you'd make it so that no lad whose father wasn't a millionaire could play at all in a really good team. For my part I see no reason why the men who make the money shouldn't have a share in the spending of it.' (THP)

But things started badly. The dismal weather had failed to clear: rain had fallen in sheets all through the morning, and the turn-out, as a result, was disastrously poor (the *Leeds Intelligencer* called it 'something even less than meagre'). Nor did the planned programme of events run smoothly. A hot-air balloon flight had to be cancelled because of the weather. The famous Lancastrian swimmer David Billington – 'Billington of Bacup' – took to the lake in a bid to break the world record for the mile – but failed. A demonstration of fire-fighting by the Low Fold Mill Brigade produced so much smoke, the *Leeds Intelligencer* reported, that no fire could be seen.

All that remained was a military tattoo, to be performed by a regiment of local reservists. But, as the part-time soldiers assembled in the mud, there can have been little prospect of their rescuing the gala. The crowd of around 10,000 must have gathered in the gloom more in hope than expectation.

At least, they must have supposed, the fireworks would brighten things up.

At around 9 p.m., technician Sidney Riley of Ossett attempted to launch a 'starburst' firework. It should have been one of the highlights of the show: on exploding, it was designed to scatter 1,000 shining coloured stars over the rainy park. But the firework never left its mortar.

Too much gunpowder had been used. What was worse, the poor-quality shellac used to coat the stars had crumbled to dust, exacerbating the risk of instability and explosion. And this was a potent cocktail indeed: in contravention of the law, the firework makers had incorporated sulphur and potassium chloride in the pyrotechnic mix.

The firework went off prematurely. The mortar shattered.

'Good heavens!' cried Gala Committee chairman N.G. Morrison. 'There's something wrong!'

He was right.

There was no fire or smoke from the blast – only a devastating shockwave that sent lethal fragments hurtling through the air. One struck Lance-Sergeant Harry Pullan of New Wortley, one of the reservists taking part in the tattoo. He fell to the floor, the left side of his face horribly mutilated. He was dead. He was twenty-three years old.

Two other young spectators, twenty-two-year-old Tom Needham and twenty-three-year-old Beatrice Tomlinson, also received lethal blows from flying shrapnel. The scene was horrendous. One young spectator was heard to ask his father: 'Is this how they fight in real war, Daddy?'

With the acrid stink of gunpowder choking the air and casualties sprawled moaning in the mud, it must indeed, as one of the reservists said, have looked 'quite like a battlefield'.

Debris from the mortar had been flung more than 400 yards by the explosion. N.G. Morrison had been narrowly missed by a chunk of shrapnel, and described the experience as 'just like a bat flying past your face'. A thirteen-year-old girl in the crowd also had a lucky escape, when a flying fragment clipped the button from her coat but left her unharmed.

Others were less lucky. 'We saw a man with his head practically blown away,' one witness told the press.

Among the casualties was James Arthur Miller, now fifty-five and a respected and long-standing member of the Yorkshire Rugby Union. He was hit in the leg, and sustained a serious compound fracture. It was doubted whether even such a tenacious character could survive the trauma.

He did so – but his leg had to be amputated.

In all, seven spectators were seriously injured in the blast.

Afterwards, it was agreed that the crowd had behaved 'splendidly'.

'There was no shrieking,' said Colonel Stead, who had been directing the tattoo, 'and no suggestion of panic.'

Fireworks expert Sidney Riley was disconsolate: 'I never thought that the mortar could burst,' he said.

There was a general feeling that an already miserable day had taken a tragic turn.

'It was a disastrous day all round,' said the mournful Mr Platt of the Leeds Lifeboat Society. 'The bad weather brought about a heavy loss, but this was nothing in comparison with the explosion, which just about filled our cup of misery to the top.'

A subsequent report by HM Inspector of Explosives condemned almost every aspect of the incident: the composition of the firework, the preparation of the mortar, the equipment used, and the management of the crowd had all been woefully inadequate.

None of which was any help to Harry Pullan, Tom Needham and Beatrice Tomlinson. Nor, for that matter, to James Arthur Miller. And Miller's misfortunes were by no means at an end.

Despite his missing leg, he remained a visible and voluble character. He continued to campaign for the supposedly pristine amateurism of rugby's early days. In 1914, he robustly condemned rugby players who had not signed up to fight in France as 'shirkers and bullet-funkers'.

But soon his own reputation would be in tatters. In 1922, he was appointed to the post of YRU Treasurer. In 1927, he was sentenced to six months in prison. In between, the court had heard, he had embezzled more than £1,000 from the Union.

He died, unremembered and unmourned, in 1939. He is buried in Lawnswood Cemetery.

AD 1941

EXPLODING MUMMIES AT THE MUSEUM

NESYAMUN THE PRIEST lived a relatively happy life. As a senior member of the clergy in the Egyptian city of Thebes during the reign of Ramesses XI, he was successful and well-respected; his workplace, the temple complex of Karnak, was one of the ancient world's most impressive sacred sites. Nesyamun rejoiced in the prestigious title of 'Keeper of the Bulls'. True, he had to eat bread that was full of grit and caused his teeth to fall out, but then so did everybody in Egypt at that time.

Even when he died, in 1100 BC, at the age of around forty, Nesyamun the priest was well looked after. He was carefully embalmed, perfumed, wrapped in the finest linen, and secured within two handsome wood coffins, each tastefully decorated with scenes from mythology.

And the next 3,000 years or so passed pretty much without incident for Nesyamun the priest.

Then he made the mistake of coming to Leeds, and everything started to go wrong.

In 1822, Nesyamun's tomb at Deir el Bahri was unearthed by an antiquarian-cum-graverobber named M.J. Passalacqua. From this point, Nesyamun was not just a dead priest – he was now archaeological hot property.

His arrival in the industrial West Riding was the work of Leeds banker John Blades, who purchased the mummified priest and presented it the Leeds Literary and Philosophical Society. Founded in 1819, the Society had the backing of some of the city's most distinguished personages: the surgeon Charles Thackrah, the industrialists John Marshall and Benjamin Gott and the newspaper proprietor Edward Baines were among the founding fathers who propelled the Society to the forefront of Leeds' cultural and intellectual life.

The Society had dabbled in Egyptology before. However, the first mummy to have his afterlife interrupted by the Society's enthusiasts had been something of a let-down when his shroud was unwrapped and it was discovered that his body had been devoured by beetles.

Nesyamun promised to be much more interesting. He arrived in Leeds in 1828. His 'unrolling' – as the semi-public unwrapping of mummies was known in those Egypt-crazy days – was attended by, among others, flax magnate

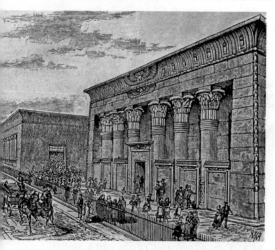

Marshall's elaborate Egyptian-styled Flax Mill, Holbeck, in around 1800. (THP)

John Marshall (Marshall was such an Egypt nut that he had the façade of his Holbeck mill constructed in the style of an Egyptian temple). Surgeon Thomas Pridgin Teale presided over the grisly scene.

As the wrappings around the dead priest's fragile body were drawn away, a smell of spices filled the room: Nesyamun had been packed in cinnamon. When, finally, the body was fully exposed, the attendant experts began their inspection. They noted that Nesyamun's nose had been squashed by the pressure of the bandages. They noted which nostril the priest's brains had been pulled out through (the right one). They were surprised to find that Nesyamun did not wear the serene and dignified facial expression generally expected of the dead – he had, in fact, been embalmed with his tongue sticking out.

It's not clear quite why Nesyamun was entombed in mid-raspberry. It may be that he had an allergic reaction to a sting or insect bite. It's also possible that he was strangled to death.

In any case, the gentleman of the Society, their pokings and pryings concluded, packed Nesyamun away again and established his sarcophagus in pride of place in their premises on Park Row. He was not alone: two other mummies who had made the trip with him from Deir el Bahri kept him company in the Society's vaults.

The mummies once again settled in for a long, peaceful rest.

But barely 100 years later – a blink of an eye when you're 3,000 years old – their repose was dramatically shattered. The war had come to Leeds.

The city's response to the outbreak of the Second World War in September 1939 was immediate. Some 16,000 air-raid shelters and around 1.5 million sandbags were prepared in anticipation of German air raids. Children and other vulnerable people were hastily evacuated to safer locations – Retford, Lincoln, Gainsborough and towns in the Yorkshire Dales all took in Leeds' evacuees.

The evacuees and their families, however, did not take kindly to being driven out of their home city: by the end of the year, most had returned to Leeds, ready to face whatever the Luftwaffe could throw at them.

Nine times the German air force pounded Leeds with incendiaries and high explosives. The most terrible assault came on the night of 14 March 1941.

The air-raid sirens sounded at 9 p.m.. The people of Leeds scurried to their bomb shelters. High overhead, the droning Luftwaffe planes unshipped their lethal cargo.

Incendiary bombs smashed into the buildings along Aire Street, by the river. The city's firemen scrambled to subdue

HISTORY REPEATING

Leeds – like every other city in Europe – had already had a taste of 'world war'. Its people had little appetite for a re-run.

And yet the city responded magnificently – just as it had done years before.

In the summer of 1914, the men of Britain signed up in their thousands to join the war against Kaiser Wilhelm's Germans, and Leeds was no exception: before the year was out, 1,275 men had enlisted with the Leeds City 'Pals' Battallion; over the course of the war, the city would provide some 82,000 fighting men.

Harewood House in the late Victorian era, just a few short years before injured men began to arrive. (THP)

Of those, more than 10,000 never came home: only 500 of the city 'Pals' lived to see the 1918 Armistice. But the heroism of the people of Leeds was not limited to the battlefields of France and Flanders. There were sacrifices to be made on the home front, too.

Military hospitals sprang up all over the city as, with the war dragging on, the casualties mounted to an appalling degree. At Beckett Street, the old workhouse became a 500-bed hospital; a new facility was opened at Chapel Allerton – but still it was not enough. All across Leeds, public buildings were pressed into service to receive the wounded: Temple Newsam House, Gledhow Hall, Roundhay Road School and Lotherton Hall all did their bit, as did temporary hospitals in Armley and Cookridge and facilities further afield in Harrogate and Thirsk.

The local aristocracy also pitched in: the Earl of Harewood volunteered his magnificent stately home in north Leeds for conversion into a hostel for convalescent soldiers.

Harewood House would again serve as a refuge for the wounded when, in 1939, war returned to Leeds.

---

the resulting blaze. The same was happening in the city centre, as fierce fires broke out in Schofield's Arcade. Water Lane was soon also ablaze. But all this was only a prelude to the Luftwaffe's main assault.

Just after midnight, a new wave of firebombs rained down on the city. The Yorkshire Post building, Mill Hill Chapel and the Royal Exchange Building all took heavy hits. Leeds' railway stations were crippled, as were the railway yards along Wellington Street. Nor did the suburbs escape the destruction: Gipton, Headingley and the Roundhay Road area were all ravaged by German incendiaries.

Then came the high explosives.

Most of the city's main landmarks were targeted: bombs fell on the Town Hall, the Infirmary, Kirkgate Market, the Quarry Hill flats, Park Square – and the Leeds Literary and Philosophical Society Park Row museum.

Thankfully, most were spared serious damage. The museum, however, was not.

The three fragile mummies had not been evacuated to the countryside or bundled into a bunker. When the bomb-blasts ripped through the museum, they never stood a chance. Two were blown apart, utterly destroyed, 3,000 years of existence brought to a devastating end. A third had its sarcophagus splintered into pieces and its nose smashed off – but it just about survived intact. This resilient third was Nesyamun, Keeper of the Bulls at the temples of Karnak.

In some ways, despite the havoc wreaked by the bombs, Leeds came through the war relatively safely. Of course, there was widespread damage and, worse, dozens of deaths – but the final toll of 77 dead, 327 injured and 197 buildings destroyed was overshadowed by the horrors that the Luftwaffe visited on cities such as Coventry, Liverpool, Sheffield and London.

German bombs had shown little respect for Leeds' long history – the ironworks at Kirkstall, begun by the 'white monks' so many centuries before, had been another of the bombers' main targets – but an ironworks, a church, a museum or a town hall can always be rebuilt. The city was battered and bruised, but it had survived.

When peace finally came on 15 August 1945, the people of Leeds danced in the streets.